"Cancel culture is coming for Christianity. In fact, as Joe Dallas observes in this timely book, it is already here. The question is not *if* it is coming, but *how* will Christians respond. I am grateful for this resource that encourages Christians to respond with wisdom, grace, and truth. I hope you will read this book and share the ideas with a friend."

Sean McDowell, PhD, professor of apologetics, Talbot School of Theology
Author of *Chasing Love: Sex, Love, and Relationships in a Confused Culture*

"Being a professing Christian who adheres to and applies the truths of Scripture to the world around us has never been easy. But today, articulating biblical precepts in the marketplace of ideas can get you fired, cancelled, censored or jailed. Joe Dallas has written what I believe may be one of the most important books you will read today. We must never be ashamed of the gospel—and we are told to proclaim its precepts. But how *do* we stand up to an increasingly hostile culture that demands our silence? How do we truly speak truth with love? Read this book to understand what winsome boldness is all about."

Janet Parshall, nationally syndicated talk show host

"Deftly written, deeply insightful, and biblically sound, this engaging book will edify, exhort, and encourage Christians in an age of confusion on contentious issues such as abortion, homosexuality, transgenderism, race, and more. I highly recommend *Christians in a Cancel Culture* to believers and unbelievers alike who desire to understand the current lies of our culture and the truths that counter those lies. Skillfully balancing grace and truth, this book shines a much-needed light in a dark world."

Becket Cook, host of *The Becket Cook Show* on YouTube
Author of *A Change in Affection: A Gay Man's Incredible Story of Redemption*

"You and I are witnessing the incremental 'criminalization' of Christianity. Don't believe it? In *Christians in a Cancel Culture*, Joe Dallas explains a number of trends growing at a frightening speed that endanger the liberties of people everywhere. His book is a worthy investment of your time. As always, Dallas provides keen analyses of his subject matter and presents you with numerous insightful conclusions. His grasp of current events, American government, the mood of present culture, and church history are all meticulous, and his research is truly educational—something that cannot be said of all people being published these days. This may very well be the most important book he has ever written."

Alex McFarland, Christian apologist
Truth for a New Generation, North Carolina

"Joe Dallas rightly dubs cancel culture a spreading madness—a virus of twisted thinking. Belief in the normalcy of the male-female sexual union is viewed as homophobic, the immutable nature of our assigned sex, transphobic, and the value of the unborn, misogynistic. The dam has burst, submerging basic Christian morality and ethics. Yet characteristically, Joe does not merely curse the darkness; he equips Christians in the art and science of conducting difficult discussions wielding the Christ-mandated gavel of grace."

Hank Hanegraaff, president, Christian Research Institute
Host of the *Bible Answer Man* broadcast and the *Hank Unplugged* podcast

"How can a Christian relationally and effectively address the cancel culture without compromising truth? That's the question so practically answered by Joe Dallas. His dialogues of likely comments and questions raised by those with a nonbiblical reference point can quickly train and equip any believer to be effectively relevant and influential, showing love and respect all along the way. This is a book long overdue and one I strongly recommend to every Christian wanting to have an impact for Christ on those around them."

Brad Dacus, Esq., President of Pacific Justice Institute

CHRISTIANS IN A CANCEL CULTURE

JOE DALLAS

HARVEST HOUSE PUBLISHERS
EUGENE. OREGON

Cover design by Faceout Studio, Jeff Miller

Cover photo © ConstantinosZ / Gettyimages; Kues / Shutterstock

Interior design by KUHN Design Group

Published in association with William K. Jensen Literary Agency, 119 Bampton Court, Eugene, Oregon 97404

For bulk, special sales, or ministry purchases, please call 1-800-547-8979.
Email: Customerservice@hhpbooks.com

M is a federally registered trademark of the Hawkins Children's LLC. Harvest House Publishers, Inc., is the exclusive licensee of the trademark.

Christians in a Cancel Culture
Copyright © 2021 by Joe Dallas
Published by Harvest House Publishers
Eugene, Oregon 97408
www.harvesthousepublishers.com

ISBN 978-0-7369-8354-9 (pbk)
ISBN 978-0-7369-8355-6 (eBook)

Library of Congress Control Number: 2021931398

Printed in the United States of America

21 22 23 24 25 26 27 28 29 / BP / 10 9 8 7 6 5 4 3 2 1

CONTENTS

X

*Peter and John answered and said to them,
"Whether it is right in the sight of God to listen to you
more than to God, you judge.
For we cannot but speak the things
which we have seen and heard."*

ACTS 4:19-20

CHAPTER ONE

THE LAST TEMPTATION

Somebody's telling you to shut up, so what are you going to do about it?

That depends. It depends on who said it, what they're telling you to quit saying, and how important you think your words are.

It starts with the *who*. If it's the government, you'll get mad and stand on your right to free speech. If it's your boss, you might be offended but still put up with it, depending on how badly you need the job. If it's a celebrity on a late-night talk show saying Christians should zip it, you might just chuckle and say, "Yeah, I really care, bro!" But if it's someone close to you, you may be hurt or bewildered, asking, "Why the hostility?" The *who* has a lot to do with your response.

As does the *what*. If someone reacts to your words, you'll ask yourself, "What did I say that got them so mad? Was it true or false? If it was true, was it appropriate? If it was true and appropriate, did I say it responsibly?" After some self-examination, you may defend, retract, explain, apologize for, or stand behind what you said.

Then comes the *how*. How important is what you're saying? Is it a hill to die on or relinquish? If it's an essential truth, you defend that hill to the end. Is it a secondary issue not worth arguing over? Then you agree to disagree. How important the issue is helps you to decide.

Those three points—the who, the what, and the how—will affect your response when someone tries to silence you. They're also the essence of what Christians consider today when responding to the demands and tactics of the Cancel Culture.

Those demands and tactics have caught us by surprise. Up until the sixties, when we talked about issues such as sexual morality, Christian orthodoxy, or abortion, we reiterated what was widely believed. Our position on those subjects was mainstream, needing little explanation and virtually no defense. It was business as usual.

Then came the social upheavals of the sixties and the sexual revolution of the seventies, and what had been commonly believed now needed to be explained to new generations with a mindset that didn't quite get where we were coming from.

By the nineties, an increasingly cynical culture compelled us to also *defend* beliefs we had just gotten used to explaining. Now Christian views weren't just seen as odd. Both they, and we who held them, were also seen as offensive, calling for a defense, not just an explanation.

But now we're having to provide a twofold defense, defending not just our beliefs, but also our right to teach and practice them. No longer viewed as a quaint group with odd ideas, we're now labeled "fascists," "haters," "bigots," and "misogynists." If someone is all that, then what else would a decent society do but tell them to shut up? Hence, the strong arm of speech codes, church disruptions, and the indignation of the "woke generation."

We're not well prepared for a fight we didn't see coming. Certainly, we knew the moral landscape was deteriorating. We knew we were having less and less influence on that landscape, and that it was drifting further every year from Judeo-Christian values. But we didn't count on it becoming downright hostile.

We should have. While we've been paying our universities six-figure tuition fees, they've been running our sons and daughters through a catechism of contempt for America, Christianity, and some of the most basic values each holds. Our media can barely conceal its bias, treating its left-leaning slant on the news as the only decent way to view current events. Our state governments have passed laws stifling religious expression and sanctioning its repression. Big Tech, that prime mover and shaker of public opinion, censors and cancels our online voices at whim while saying, with a wink and a smirk, "We value free speech. We just want to protect our community!"

That's the big picture, but there's a smaller one causing us even more turmoil. In our own families, social connections, places of work, and spheres of influence, we're feeling at an intimate level the tensions being played out nationally.

People who are most dear to us are becoming strangers to us, not by our choice but by their disgust with our views and, as a result, their dismissal of us. In most cases, their designation of us as "untouchables" is a reaction to our beliefs about homosexuality, transgenderism, race, abortion, salvation, judgment, and sin nature. Our crime is not the adoption of those beliefs but our refusal to abandon them, as the truly enlightened folks seem to have done.

The culture is embracing a new world vision, but we haven't. So we're charged with refusal to bend, and now, shocked and numbed by our recent arrest, we're prepping for the trial.

It can be held anywhere we converse and interact. Gone are the days of Bible-believing Christians living an unchallenged faith, because the land we once viewed as a comfortable home is becoming foreign territory, barely recognizable to those of us who remember other times.

Are we ready?

Ready or not, here comes the mandate to face the cancel culture, hear its charges against us, and do something perhaps new to us but historically common to the church: be ready to give an answer for the hope that lies within us (1 Peter 3:15), speak the truth in love (Ephesians 4:15), be unashamed of our Master's words (Luke 9:26), act as ambassadors for Christ (2 Corinthians 5:20), and contend earnestly for the faith once delivered to the saints (Jude 3).

My own work since 1987, as a biblical counselor and Christian speaker addressing sexual issues, has forced me to do just that. Early on, I realized I wouldn't be allowed to just minister to people who wanted to reject sexual sin. I'd also have to articulate a defense for their decision, and mine as well, both as a counselor to them and an advocate for their choice.

That meant sharpening tools and weapons at the same time. Tools were needed to minister, but weapons were also needed to defend. They included a working knowledge of the arguments being used against us, a "wise as serpents" approach to public dialogue, and the covering of intercessors. It meant going to boot camp and battle at the same time, learning as you go. Anyone who has served on the front lines of culturally edgy ministry will tell you the same.

But these days, the lines between civilians and soldiers are awfully fuzzy. Any one of us who believes in the authority of Scripture, its relevance to social issues, and the importance of offering a defense for sound doctrine will find herself or himself drafted into battle. Just say "Let there be light," and watch the darkness howl.

We know where we stand. The question becomes, *How* do we stand? How do we not only articulate the biblical view on today's controversies, but also defend that view against serious, false, but widely believed accusations?

This book was written in hopes of answering the "How do we stand?" question when we as Christians are charged with homophobia, sexism, racism, transphobia, and judgmentalism. At some point, you're likely to be accused of one or all of the above, and you'll need to give an answer.

KEEP THE FAITH, LOSE THE OFFENSE

You'll need to give an answer not only in response to the culture's challenge, but also in response to what may become one of the church's last major temptations—the temptation to minimize the importance of doctrines that are critical to the faith but offensive to the world.

Now, some of what we believe and express is acceptable to the culture. You can say, "I love Jesus" just about anywhere without serious pushback. You can quote Psalm 23 on social media, sing a hymn during your office break, or publicly thank the Lord when you accept your Grammy. Do any of these, and you're not likely to find your career threatened, your Facebook page taken down, or your human decency questioned. In these kinds of ways, professing Christianity is generally acceptable.

But professing certain Christian doctrines is not, and there's the rub. It is not a vaguely defined faith that's getting people into hot water. It's Christian distinctives, beliefs about life and people that are spelled out in both the Old and New Testaments yet tempting to downplay in these times of easy offense and swift retaliation.

All of which can leave us asking if perhaps we can keep the faith but lose the offense. Why, after all, should we alienate people? If certain biblical truths drive unbelievers away from us (and our churches), then shouldn't we avoid those and concentrate instead on just loving people, sharing the gospel, and being good neighbors? According to polls, Christians have a credibility problem. The world allegedly sees us as judgmental, unloving, anti-women, anti-gay, anti-trans, and anti-progress. So shouldn't we water down some of our positions to gain back the trust we seem to have lost?

This is where I fear the desire to get along is superseding the desire to obey. When God instructed the people of Israel on how they were to function in their new land, He placed obedience above all else. He also gave His priests a mandate that we, as members of a holy priesthood (1 Peter 2:5), would do well to consider:

> ...that you may distinguish between holy and unholy, and
> between unclean and clean (Leviticus 10:10).

This mandate to distinguish between the two was reiterated through Ezekiel:

> They shall teach My people the difference between the holy
> and the unholy, and cause them to discern between the
> unclean and the clean. In controversy they shall stand as
> judges, and judge it according to my judgments. They shall
> keep My laws and My statutes in all My appointed meet-
> ings, and they shall hallow My sabbaths (Ezekiel 44:23-24).

God expected those who were leading His people to make the distinction between right and wrong, normal and abnormal, clean versus unclean. When controversy arose, these leaders were to consult God's judgments, not the polls. Obtaining the approval of the surrounding culture had little to do with their job description.

Likewise, though modern believers have no mandate to force biblical morality onto nonbelievers (1 Corinthians 5:12), we are obligated to hold fast to that morality, practice it ourselves, teach it in our homes and churches, and express it when expedient. To be asked, for example, "Where do you stand on abortion?" provides an opportunity for dialogue and an obligation to honesty. The fear of controversy, though understandable, is no excuse for evasion when truth is called for.

Then again, modern Christians aren't necessarily rewriting the Bible to accommodate abortion, homosexuality, or transgenderism. Some are, but when they do, they embrace errors so glaring that most biblically grounded believers see the errors for what they are and reject them.

But others embrace something not so easily discerned. It's not a wholesale revision of truth, but a minimizing of its importance. That minimizing, often done in the name of keeping peace, is an easier error to fall into than blatant heresy, a fact making it especially dangerous. It's a siren call to keep the faith but lose the offense, often for the sake of achieving a goal through a pragmatic but serious compromise.

In that sense, perhaps the challenge is nothing new. Luke's account of Christ being tempted by Satan (Luke 4:1-13) describes a similar challenge. Read the passage through, then think again about the specific offers Satan made to Jesus. They seem to boil down to this: "You have a mission to save humanity. OK, fine, let's make it easier. I'll give You the world and its people if You'll excise a few items from Your job description, like that ugly cross business. Worship me, skip the suffering, and they're all Yours. Unsaved and eternally lost, sure, but a nice and orderly kingdom. Just remove the truths that make it hard, and You can have it all."

Today's enticement to modern Christianity seems awfully similar. "Just compromise those distinctives we take issue with, and you can be the church that gets along smoothly with the world."

Problem is, it's a world under the same influencer who tempted Christ, as per Paul's identification centuries ago when he cited him as "the prince of the power of the air, the spirit who now works in the sons of disobedience" (Ephesians 2:2). It's also a world that says to us, somewhat as its influencer said to Him, "You Christians have a mission to evangelize humanity? OK, that's fine, let's make it easier. You see how much trouble you get into for saying and believing the wrong things? You can be spared all that if you'll mute a few items in your belief system. Like that rigid definition of marriage, the divinely assigned male or female status, the insistence that life in the womb is in fact life in the womb, the refusal to acknowledge there are different ways to God, that belief in a place of eternal punishment, and that insulting doctrine about people being born sinful rather than wonderful. You don't have to deal with laws passed against you, or censorship imposed on you, or friends and loved ones rejecting you. We can all get along! Just minimize the truths that make it hard, and you can have it all."

But think again about whether those truths are negotiable. They include the exclusive nature of salvation as coming only through Christ's atonement and faith in Him, the Creator's definition of marriage and sexuality, the command to perpetuate the race rather than murder its future unborn members, the recognition of sin and its consequences, and the concept of individual responsibility rather than the indictment of an entire race as being guilty of a sin by virtue of its race alone.

Remove these from the Christian faith, and you're left with something akin to what Satan hoped Christ would accept: a false, incomplete, and wholly inadequate version of what the Father sent Him to redeem, and an abortion not only of what that Father intended Him to do, but what He Himself declared His goal to be: to seek and save the lost.

Had Christ said yes to this temptation, He would surely have said no to us in the same breath, as a civilization packaged for Him without redemption would have been the very thing God prevented by driving a fallen Adam and Eve from the garden lest they eat from the tree of life and remain always and forever unredeemed (Genesis 3:22).

Likewise, if we say yes to this modern temptation, what are we offering the world if not a neutered church, an ineffective gospel, a place to gather nicely but receive limited truth, and the bleak achievement of approval coming from those we were meant to reach, not just please?

No, we're not likely to be opposed, limited, or persecuted for merely expressing our belief in God. Our belief in His words is another matter, a point He Himself made when He admonished that those who are not only ashamed of Him but of His teachings as well are subject to His displeasure (Luke 9:26).

All of which leaves us with this hard and increasingly unavoidable question: Will we faithfully—in our pulpits, homes, and lives—profess and steward the Word of God without adding to or detracting from it? Or will we acquiesce when the world enticingly reminds us that a profession of something less than the whole counsel of God will allow us a far more peaceful though far less profitable existence?

THAT'S WHY WE'RE TALKING

Those are the reasons you and I will be required to give an answer, and those are the reasons this book was written.

It was not written, however, to provide guidance in resisting social media censorship, unjust anti-Christian legislation, or government interference. There is a huge need for such guidance, but this is not the place to look for it.

This was written with a more personal goal in mind: that of equipping believers to provide reasonable answers and have effective dialogue with family members, close friends, and associates who take issue with their belief system.

So in chapters 1–5, I've tried to frame the issues with some background and context. In chapters 6–10, we will look at the hot topics with an overview of each, along with the reasons for seeing these as primary rather than secondary doctrinal issues, some rules of engagements to follow, and talking points to use when you're conversing. In chapter 11, we will consider where we're going and how to take one last stand along the way.

I've learned much these past three decades about taking such a stand, and I've still much to learn about speaking truth in a time of confusion. Yet however dark and confusing the times may be, I'm more convinced than ever that the Word of God is still the answer, and that it remains exactly what it's always claimed to be.

It is *alive.* "The word of God is living and powerful, and sharper than any two-edged sword, piercing even to the division of soul and spirit, and of the joints and marrow, and is a discerner of the thoughts and intents of the heart" (Hebrews 4:4).

It is *relevant.* "All Scripture is given by inspiration of God, and is profitable for doctrine, for reproof, for correction, for instruction in righteousness, that the man of God may be complete, thoroughly equipped for every good work" (2 Timothy 3:16-17).

It is *potent.* "So shall My word be that goes forth from My mouth; it shall not return to Me void, but it shall accomplish what I please, and it shall prosper in the thing for which I sent it" (Isaiah 55:11).

I am grateful to Harvest House Publishers for their thirty years of support and friendship, and to William Jensen of the William A. Jensen Literary Agency for helping me appreciate both the need and the timing of this book.

I hope you will find it to be an encouraging and useful tool.

CHAPTER TWO

OF RAVERS
AND CAVERS

Joan Rivers peered at me as if I were an obnoxious insect. She was too professional to swat me, but so against what I stood for that her disdain, though controlled, was clear.

The comedienne had invited me onto her daytime talk show in the early nineties to discuss whether or not gays can change. I was there to say yes; the other guests were an openly gay couple who were there to say no, and neither Miss Rivers nor her New York City studio audience made any bones about their sympathies. By the time the cameras turned to me, it was clear who were the lions and who was the lunch.

Before the interview, the gay guests were put up in the luxurious Plaza Hotel. I was placed in a nice little room down the street. They were chauffeured to the studio; I was given directions to walk. They were hosted before the show in the Green Room; I was left alone to wait in a cubby on the far side of the building. Miss Rivers introduced them to applause; I was introduced to icy silence.

It was no surprise. Although I was new to the game, having only been in ministry a couple years, I'd heard plenty of stories about media bias and the hits so often taken by conservative Christians when they did interviews. Still, disparity in guest treatment is hardly the stuff martyrs are made of, and, after all, I had agreed to do the interview without any expectation of a red carpet.

Yet the message was clear—I was the theologically conservative Bozo, a point borne home each time I interacted with any member of Miss Rivers's staff before going on air. So by the time she turned to me on camera with a cross-examination about my views, I knew where I stood, and I knew I was among people who didn't like where I stood.

What I didn't know was how on earth, under those circumstances, I should *explain* where I stood.

So I took a deep breath.

X

Today's Christians are wondering whether or not to say what they believe, how to say it when they do, and how to handle a backlash that keeps getting meaner and less reasonable. Facing a culture, friends, or even family members who are hostile to their beliefs, they know where they stand, and they know they're often among people who don't like where they stand. They, too, are taking a deep breath.

If you breathe, you believe; if you believe, you express. Those two facts aren't going to change anytime soon.

Everyone believes. That's why you figure some things are true, others are false, and daily, while looking at people and events around you, you say to yourself, "That's good" or "Now, that's just wrong!" As surely as we have to die and pay taxes, we have to believe. We are believers by nature.

Expressers too. What we believe, we will also consider expressing, and that's where things can get dicey. Because that's when what we are about to say goes through a committee.

That mental committee of ours (often called our "filter") holds a discussion over how controversial our expression will be and what consequences it might bring. It weighs things such as friendship status, job security, embarrassment, risk of offending, reputation, and the virtue or the vice of causing a scene. Above all, it considers our primary goal: what we hope to accomplish by expressing what we believe.

The committee decides, we take a deep breath, then we declare. According to the committee's recommendation, we declare what we believe, or we declare a lie by denying what we believe. Or maybe we'll opt to declare a watered-down version of what we believe, or even become defensive and declare what we believe aggressively. Then again, we might just plead the Fifth because that seems prudent, or safe, or both.

Ideally, the environment we're in will be reasonable enough that the committee's job won't be too hard. In that case, we'll express ourselves, beliefs and feelings included, in the context of mature conversations. When we say, "I believe *this*," we may be disagreed with or even challenged by those who believe *that*. But when everyone's behaving fairly (read "like adults"), then declaring our beliefs won't trigger serious relational, professional, or legal consequences.

But our cultural landscape is becoming less reasonable and more risky because this is the age of the Tantrum, not the Adult. Worse, it's the age of the Uzi-Toting Tantrum, the kind that not only says, "Your views are wrong" or even "Your views make you an idiot." Rather, the UTT says, "Your views make you dangerous and repugnant, therefore you must be punished, your views must be silenced, and your voice must be cancelled."

Plenty of modern Christians are feeling the Cancel Culture's Uzi. Some notice it when a coworker learns they go to church and asks them loudly, in the middle of a crowded break room, "So are you against a woman's right to choose?" Others feel it when their non-Christian supervisor corners them at the Christmas office party with the accusative question, "Are you really saying people can't go to heaven without Jesus?"

Parents face the Uzi when their lesbian daughter demands an explanation for their reluctance to attend her same-sex wedding, threatening to cut them off if they decline. Students face it when their university professor shames them in front of the class for not affirming LGBTQ rights, lowering both their grade and their campus status. Christian employees know they're in its sights when the male-to-female transgender individual in the next cubicle says, "From now on, you'd better call me Elizabeth. You'll be hearing from management if you don't."

Pastors being interviewed on secular TV shows can almost taste the muzzle when the host leans forward and asks, with arched eyebrows, "So you really believe people who don't think like you do are headed for a lake of fire?" Members of social media feel it when they see posts declaring that their race makes them a racist in need of repentance, re-education, and lifelong penance. And many of us feel it when we try explaining the "all have sinned" verses to a friend who huffs, "I think I'm wonderful not sinful, I think you're a hater, and I think you're unfriended!"

These days, if you take Jesus at His word when He claims to be the only way to God, or if you believe there is a literal hell awaiting the unrighteous, or if you hold to the Judeo-Christian definition of marriage and family, or if you believe we are male or female without a curtain number 3, or if you believe racism is an evil shown by words and actions rather than color, or if you believe life in the womb is in fact life in the womb, or if you believe people are born sinful rather than fabulous, then you're a candidate for backlash.

It may come as a notice of suspension from Facebook, a broken relationship, a lawsuit, a firing, cancelled contracts, or loss of credentials, all of which are happening to Christians everywhere who simply express their beliefs.

That's why, these days, our committees are scrambling to keep up. We simply don't know what's OK to say, what to keep to ourselves, and what's the difference between wise discretion and plain old cowardliness.

Plenty of non-Christians are facing this dilemma too, of course. A person's views on immigration, racism, socialism, or party affiliation can start a riot, so people of all faiths, or no faith, are feeling the heat.

But it's a heat posing a twofold challenge to Christians. Like our secular friends, we're obliged to answer the culture when it asks, "Why do you believe that?" But unlike secular apologists, we don't just answer the culture. We answer to God, not only for what we say, but for how we say it. So when people get scary, we don't get to cave. When people get obnoxious, we don't get to rave.

Certainly, if the situation doesn't call for an unvarnished declaration of hard truth regardless of consequences, then we can be as discreet as we please. But when our backs are against the wall and compromise would be a sin, then disciples aren't given a choice between expressing grace or truth. We can only show both.

TO SEEK AND TO SAVE, NOT TO SQUEAK OR TO RAVE

Christians feeling heat from the Cancel Culture may also feel a pull toward one of two extremes: the wrath of man or the fear of man.

"The wrath of man," James warned, "does not produce the righteousness of God" (James 1:20). Wrath doesn't want to correct a wrongdoing. It only wants to punish the wrongdoer, in direct contradiction to the heart of God, which rejoices in mercy, not judgment (James 2:13).

But the fear of man is no better, because according to the Proverbs, "The fear of man brings a snare" (Proverbs 29:25). Believers who let cultural intimidation keep them silent wind up ensnared by their own fears, afraid of offending man more than God, keeping peace at the cost of integrity.

Jesus modeled the better way. He was neither a timid, squeaking mouse who scurried from confrontation, nor a raving loudmouth who built a following with insults and sarcasm. He was, as John said, full of grace and truth (John 1:4). John later mentioned that if we say we know Him, we should also walk as He walked (1 John 2:6). If we do, we'll avoid both extremes.

So said Paul, in what must be the most succinct job description on record for anyone wanting to serve God: "And a servant of the Lord must not quarrel but be gentle to all, able to teach, patient, in humility correcting those who are in opposition, if God perhaps will grant them repentance, so that they may know the truth" (2 Timothy 2:24-25).

A follower of Christ, then, must not strive. Trolling for social media fights won't get you hired, and "gentle to all," "patient," and "in humility" also make it clear that in God's service, contention junkies need not apply.

Of course, just as Jesus said some eunuchs are born that way and others are made that way (Matthew 19:12), I wonder if the same principle doesn't apply to ravers. For some, it seems to be in their genes; for others, nurture clearly played a hand.

We've all known women and men who must have popped out of the womb calling the OB an idiot and threatening a lawsuit over that slap. They've always loved a good fight, and they're forever finding or starting one. The noted atheist Madeline Murray O'Hare, who went on record saying how much she enjoyed a brawl, comes to mind. So does the late talk-show host Wally George, who in the eighties made a living out of hard-right political buffoonery. Their offspring can be seen today in the bloggers, talking heads, and politicians who emulate their abrasiveness, buoyed by millions of fans who, like schoolyard kids hearing someone yell "Fight!," clamor to see and hear the action.

But ravers can also be made, and the times we're in just might, if we're not careful, make them out of otherwise reasonable people. Push folks too far, and even the nicest ones get mad, sometimes ravingly so. This, I fear, is a temptation more and more believers could succumb to.

Consider the shattered Canadian father who was ordered by the courts to stop referring to his fourteen-year-old daughter who desired to transition from female to male as "she" because, the judge declared, doing so "shall be considered to be family violence."[1] Watch the video of pro-life teenaged girls gathered for prayer outside Planned Parenthood as they're heckled and harassed by State Senator Brian Sims of Pennsylvania, who interrupts them and offers, on camera, $100 to anyone who'll "dox" (publicly identify or publish private information about someone, such as their home address) the girls.[2] Or better yet, check out the video of an eighty-five-year-old pro-life gentleman being thrown to the ground and kicked by a young San Francisco thug who relishes his power, warning his elderly victim, "Stay on the ground, old man, unless you want to get hurt!"[3]

Just writing about this makes me feel a bit violent, and that's how ravers get made. Nazis can turn pacifists into resistance fighters, and not the nice kind. I made that morph myself one night almost thirty years ago when I faced an auditorium full of shouting, raging AIDS activists.

I'd been invited to give an evening talk at the University of Utah in Salt Lake City. It was a free event, heavily promoted on campus, and a number of groups combined their efforts to protest and disrupt. So when I was introduced and took the stage, I saw row after row of black T-shirts with pink triangles topped by angry faces. I was scheduled to speak for a solid hour, then take questions. Good luck with that.

The sharks were hangry. I would get perhaps three sentences out, then someone would yell, "Ridiculous!," "Bigoted!," or "You're not qualified to say that!" It went on and on, me spurting out a few lines, them screaming interruptions, me struggling for composure.

Fifteen minutes into this fiasco I glanced at the front row, where the only people in the auditorium who didn't want to dissect me were seated. The university security guards were shrugging as if to say, "We can't do anything about this." The pastors who hosted me were leaning forward as if to say, "We're glad we're down here." My wife, seated next to the pastors, looked at me as if to say, "Who do you want for your pallbearers?"

The stupidity of it all had me steaming. This was allegedly a place of higher education, where alleged adults were sharpening their alleged intelligence. Worse yet, these people were allegedly supporters of diversity, tolerance, pluralism. I didn't mind their disagreement; I didn't resent their hostility. But I couldn't stomach their childish, brazen hypocrisy, not to mention their cowardly bullying.

I'd prayed long and hard about this talk, spending most of the day preparing it, convinced God had given me some important points to make. I so wanted to make them in the right spirit.

But then I didn't. Enough Mr. Rogers; let's try some Jack Nicholson. I'm a quiet man who is nonetheless, I say with all due modesty, blessed with a terrific shouting voice. When I let it rip, I'll match my volume against any radical. So I stepped back, inhaled, and there she blew: *"If you people can't act like adults and quit this stupid brainless screaming, then you can sit here and throw your tantrums all night, but to hell with all of you. I'm outta here!"*

My decibels could beat up their decibels. It got quiet. Bullies never can hold their own when they're challenged. In that moment of silence I told myself I'd won, but surely, I had lost.

I lost because at that point, rather than moving ahead redemptively, I got drunk with power. My chest puffed, my eyes blazed, and I was suddenly the Man, all mouth and no ministry, shouting platitudes and bumper sticker sayings but going completely off script from what God had laid it on my heart to say. I raved, and I accomplished nothing. It might as well have been a WWE match.

Reacting to the extreme measures Cancel Culture takes against the Christian voice (measures a hundred times worse than the heckling I was getting that night), some Christians may forget that the weapons of our warfare are not carnal (2 Corinthians 10:4). That can lead to a whole new set of weapons and a whole new kind of war.

When we're pushed too far, it's easy to respond by raving and come out swinging. That's when we lose interest in winning others to Christ. Instead, we just get hooked on winning, rhetorically and politically.

Which feels good, for sure. Tasting the adrenaline of contention can make you thirsty for another cup, and sooner than you realize, you're so caught up in beating the other side that you quit the race you were supposed to run and join a quarrel you were never called to.

Ravers win, occasionally, but they never, never prosper. "Do not be overcome by evil," Paul reminds us, "but overcome evil with good" (Romans 12:21).

WHEN "NICE" ISN'T

Yet "good" doesn't always mean "nice," and the believer who makes niceness his primary goal is in danger of becoming a caver.

That's especially true since the meaning of "nice" shifts so often. The word used to mean polite and warm, a combination of friendliness and respect, but not anymore. Today niceness isn't just about attitude, it's about positions. More to the point, it's about holding the right positions and openly rejecting the wrong ones, right and wrong being defined by the cultural elite who are good enough to keep us informed.

If you ignore their memos by holding on to unacceptable views, then no matter how kindly you express them, no matter how careful your wording, no matter how soft your tone, you can't wear the "nice" hat.

Besides, too much niceness doesn't have impact. It's hard for people to respect, much less take seriously, anyone who's trying so hard to be nice that he compromises his beliefs for the sake of getting along.

But we do want to get along, and there's nothing wrong in that. In most cases, actually, it's commendable.

First, it's biblical. "As much as depends on you," Paul wrote, "live peaceably with all men" (Romans 12:18). The Proverbs commend deescalating an argument with kindness by advising, "A soft answer turns away wrath" (Proverbs 15:1). They also encourage showing friendliness to others in order to gain friends (Proverbs 18:24). Jesus had Peter fish for a coin to pay taxes to avoid offending people (Matthew 17:27), and Paul circumcised Timothy to ensure better relations with Jewish citizens (Acts 16:1-5). Getting along, then, has biblical precedent.

Besides which, the friendly respect Christians show to non-Christians—evidenced in our tone, humor, and affection—not only honors our God but sweetens our message. People are more receptive to truth when they've first been shown consideration.

Second, it's human. As social creatures we are, and should be, inclined to connect. Every aspect of life works better when we're getting along, recognizing and respecting differences. The efficiency of the office, the athletic team, the classroom, or the church staff has much to do with how well the people involved treat each other, a point so basic it hardly needs to be made.

Except it does need to be made because it's been largely forgotten, and that's bad news for all of us. It can't end well for a civilization without civility, a fact many of us are more than a little worried about. That's why there was such widespread delight in the fall of 2019 when Ellen DeGeneres tweeted a defense of her friendliness toward President George W. Bush, after someone snapped a shot of her and her partner seated with the Bushes at a Dallas Cowboys game.[4]

The sight of a lesbian icon enjoying a ballgame with a conservative

Republican president was encouraging to millions of Americans grown weary of the culture wars, and wearier still with the partisan refusal by too many citizens and leaders to see the value of unity and the virtue of friendliness being extended across the aisle. Getting along is a worthy goal and a healthy desire.

But caving is neither. To cave is not just to get along. It's to value getting along above all else, even at the expense of honesty, integrity, or higher loyalties. Caving happens when a need for approval or an aversion to conflict or a fear of consequence overrides convictions. It's inevitable when the fear of man takes over, a fear which, as Proverbs 29:25 observes, "brings a snare."

That snare has been making public appearances lately as high-profile Christians have shown more and more reluctance to give straight answers on vital issues they know will raise controversy.

Now some issues can bear some hemming and hawing. If I was asked on national television where I stood on the pretribulation rapture of the church or the question of eternal security, I'd allow myself enough leeway to say, "Well, here's my position, but there's a variety of opinion on this, and there's room for disagreement since these aren't doctrinal essentials."

But some issues—the divinity of Christ, the definition of marriage, or the sanctity of preborn life, for example—may be a little scary to talk about, but they're also essential. When asked about these, there's no room for the steward of truth to be coy.

Sadly, though, coyness is an option too often taken. When Hillsong's New York City pastor Carl Lentz, for example, was a guest on the popular women's show *The View*, host Joy Behar asked whether or not his church considered abortion a sin. He responded: "Um, that's the kind of conversation we would have finding out your story, where you're from, what you believe. I mean, God's the Judge, people have to live with their own convictions."[5]

In fairness to Lentz, he also, on another occasion, openly condemned a New York law making it legal to terminate an unborn child up to the last day of pregnancy. He not only criticized the law, he also called it "shameful and demonic,"[6] though he wasn't on *The View* when he said that. Yet while holding deep convictions on preborn life, his committee seems to have found those convictions too hot to state plainly amidst *The View's* pro-choice, feminist environment.

When Grammy-award-winning Christian artist Lauren Daigle was in a similar situation, she responded in a similar way. Asked during a radio interview if she considered homosexuality a sin, she replied:

> I can't honestly answer on that. In a sense, I have too many people that I love that are homosexual. I don't know. I actually had a conversation with someone last night about it. I can't say one way or the other. I'm not God. So when people ask questions like that…that's what my go-to is. I just say read the Bible and find out for yourself. And when you find out let me know, because I'm learning too.[7]

One wonders if we're not letting the world tell us which sins to condemn and which ones not to touch. Imagine, for example, Joy Behar asking Pastor Lentz if his church considered sexism a sin, then imagine him saying, in response: "Um, that's the kind of conversation we would have finding out your story, where you're from, what you believe. I mean, God's the Judge, people have to live with their own convictions."

Or Miss Daigle, in response to a question of whether racism is a sin:

> I can't honestly answer on that. In a sense, I have too many people that I love that are racist. I don't know. I actually had a conversation with someone last night about it. I can't say one way or the other. I'm not God. So when people ask questions like that…that's what my go-to is. I just say read the Bible and find out for yourself. And when you find out let me know, because I'm learning too.

Unthinkable? Only because we're saluting, more than we probably know, our culture's hierarchy and catalogue of sins. Some are heinous and demand outrage, others are minimal, and others are…well, they're no longer sins at all.

Hence we cave, not only by refusing clarity when it's called for, but by accepting the world's counsel on which sins we may openly classify and which practitioners of sin we must openly pacify.

But hey, I've got no first stone to cast here, because when I was Joan River's guest back in 1990, I committed every sin I just critiqued.

I'd flown to New York City wanting only to build bridges, show the audience not all Christians were homophobic, share my concern over the way some Christian leaders at the time were trashing gays and lesbians, and as a former member of the gay community, I wanted to be Mr. Nice Guy, expressing good will and hoping for peaceful coexistence.

Actually, those goals weren't so bad. But they never should have been so *primary*. Truth first; niceness second, I've learned since then. Winsomeness is fine, but never the main goal.

With priorities skewed, no wonder I did poorly. When Joan asked me about the reported failure of ministries like mine, I tried way too hard to be magnanimous instead of defending the value of any ministry helping people pursue God's will for their sexuality. When a studio guest asked me what homosexuality was, instead of calling it a sin, I called it a "variation of human sexuality." When asked about my own sexual history, because I knew some of my family members weren't comfortable with me making my testimony too public, I deflected, saying I preferred not to talk about that in public . (How naïve can you get?) I certainly didn't say "gay was good" and, in fact, I clarified that I didn't hold to any interpretation of the Bible that justified homosexuality. Still, given the chance to state plainly that God created us for male-female union, and that many of us who once embraced homosexuality have now joyfully embraced His created intent, I faltered, alternating between defensive and apologetic.

A REASON FOR REFORM

So nobody needs to tell me how easy it is to cave under the hot lights, atop the hot seat, before a national audience. Your mental committee assesses the situation and argues, "Let's be liked; let's be nice; let's look good," then votes for concession. It's wrong but understandable. I've been there and I know.

Thankfully, I've also had countless interview and speaking opportunities since 1990 and have learned to speak with much more balance and clarity along the way. Practice makes better. Never perfect, but certainly improved. For that I'm grateful.

As for raving and caving, I'll plead guilty to both, while recognizing I have some good company.

To his everlasting regret, Peter caved when he denied knowing Jesus (Luke 22:54-62). To his shorter-lived regret, poor Moses raved when he struck the rock God told him to merely speak to, costing him his life and entrance into the Promised Land (Numbers 20:10-12).

But understandable as both extremes are, they can be avoided, and they must. Our ability to fulfill the Great Commission depends on it. Remember Jesus' final instructions:

> "Go therefore and make disciples of all the nations, baptizing them in the name of the Father and of the Son and of the Holy Spirit, teaching them to observe all things that I have commanded you; and lo, I am with you always, even to the end of the age" (Matthew 28:19-20).

That's a mandate to preach the gospel and make converts, then teach those converts the Word and make disciples.

To preach the gospel we have to speak the truth about man's sinful state and his need for salvation, the promise Jesus made as the only way to the Father, and the eternal consequences for rejecting His offer.

To make disciples we have to instruct them in sound doctrine, which is, according to Paul, profitable for "instruction in righteousness" (2 Timothy 3:16). That instruction includes teaching the truth about marriage, the sanctity of life, sexuality, gender, and what personal responsibility means and entails. If we allow Cancel Culture to keep us from teaching these basics, we'll cancel our own ability to fulfill our commission.

Tim Keller, acknowledging this very thing, warns against removing key doctrinal points, while underscoring the absurdity of professing the faith and dismantling it at the same time:

If something is truly integral to a body of thought, you can't remove it without destabilizing the whole thing. A religion can't be whatever we desire it to be. If I'm a member of the board of Greenpeace and I come out and say climate change is a hoax, they will ask me to resign. I could call them narrow-minded, but they would rightly say that there have to be some boundaries for dissent or you couldn't have a cohesive, integrated organization. And they'd be right. It's the same with any religious faith.[8]

Without adherence to Scripture we'll never have a cohesive, integrated church. If all Scripture really is inspired of God, meant to be used by His servants to teach and correct (2 Timothy 3:16), and if, by knowing it and using it properly, women and men of God become mature and equipped for every good work (2 Timothy 3:17), then surely we are mandated to know, express, and when necessary, defend all of Scripture. Refuse that mandate by acknowledging only some of the Bible but avoiding some of it as well, and you cripple the impact of its whole by minimizing the sacred imperatives in its parts.

Martin Luther made no bones about that:

If I profess with the loudest voice and clearest exposition every portion of the truth of God except precisely that little point which the world and the devil are at the moment attacking, I am not confessing Christ, however boldly I may be professing Christ. *Where the battle rages, there the loyalty of the soldier is proved.* And to be steady on all the battle fields besides is merely flight and disgrace if he flinches at that point (emphasis mine).[9]

A battle over truth is raging, not just over the nature of truth, but the right to speak it as well. Only this time it's not, as Luther said, one "little point" under attack. It's several points, points fundamental to our understanding of Christian living. But he was right about the loyalty of the soldier. It's being proven as each of us decides to meet, or avoid, the challenge to speak truthfully and lovingly, compromising neither.

So we can rave, giving such offense that we cause our own silencing. Or we can cave, avoiding all offense and inviting our own silencing.

Either way, if we become complicit with the Cancel Culture in its goal to silence our voice on vital but unpopular doctrine, then we'll set a precedent by which the church says to the world, "We hereby give you permission to dictate to us which truths we may speak and which truths we must avoid."

That's when the church will abdicate her role as the light of the world, and the world will assume its role as the light of the church.

CHAPTER THREE

YOU'VE BEEN SERVED

If we accept our responsibility to avoid raving or caving, we should better understand what it is we need to avoid raving about or caving in to. This level of intolerance we're seeing is just the latest evolution of something that's been brewing for years, manifesting itself now as the Cancel Culture.

But years before it morphed into that, it was an alternative culture that took a seat at the table, asking for tolerance. For a while it sat with us genially (remember those sweet "Coexist" bumper stickers?) while growing in numbers and shoring up allies, a proverbial kettle of warm water ready to boil the unsuspecting frog.

It evolved. The last few decades have witnessed those pleas for tolerance become demands for uniformity. Celebrations of diversity have become declarations of war against anything deemed bigoted or hateful, the meaning of those terms being decided at the whims of self-appointed elites. What used to be liberal has shifted to a rigid Puritanism that won't be reasoned with, only obeyed or defied, eager to hang whoever it fingers as a witch.

We're now in the final act. If you've seen the play, you know that's when the Phantom of the Opera finally unmasks.

So he has, a looming figure we call the Cancel Culture, which isn't an easily defined term. Sometimes it refers to the online censuring or boycotting of a person, group, or business that has said something offensive.[1] Sometimes it means the official cancelling of a person's job or career;[2] other times it means groups (read "mobs") intimidating perceived offenders, tearing down statues, rioting, or demanding that historical figures be written out of history.[3]

The definition of Cancel Culture found in the *Cambridge Dictionary* is useful, if incomplete: "A way of behaving in a society or group, especially on social media, in which it is common to completely reject and stop supporting someone because they have said or done something that offends you."[4]

That comes close, but it omits the punitive nature of Cancel Culture. Most of us who get cancelled wouldn't mind if that only meant we'd been "rejected," or that someone "stopped supporting" us, or that a family member or friend simply disagreed with us. Too often, though, cancelled really means silenced, forcibly shut down, or completely cut off by a friend or loved one.

Cambridge hints at that punitive nature when it elaborates on its definition of Cancel Culture with some example quotes:

> "Let's call cancel culture what it really is: it is our way to exert some control over a world that is increasingly becoming more dangerous and less tolerant."

> "Cancel culture has its place—it helps to call out and remove problematic people from mainstream culture."

> "In a cancel culture, we appoint ourselves the arbiters of right and wrong and also the judge and jury, because thanks to social media, we get to dole out punishment."[5]

This term, like "politically correct," can be used unfairly. If someone objects to a crude remark I made, I might cry "Cancel Culture!" or "Political correctness!" to deflect from my wrongdoing by criticizing my critics, rather than giving their complaints a fair hearing.

But it is fair to say Cancel Culture is our new French Revolution clamoring to behead anyone deemed an aristocrat, drunk with the power to tear down but not at all sure what it wants to build up.

"Revolution," though, may not be the best word for it. Granted, its goals are revolutionary, and its tactics can show the brutality of a merciless takeover. Look closer, though, and I think you'll see something more like a virus than a revolution.

Revolutions usually have centralized leadership and definable goals. You know who's behind them, pulling the strings, financing the movement, and giving the marching orders. While plenty of speculations may spread about figures, groups, or nations orchestrating all of this, the fact is that if there are such conductors, as of this writing, neither their identification nor the roles they're playing have been verified.

Viruses are more subtle, spreading and infecting millions who aren't otherwise connected, but all of whom show the symptoms. That's why I see Cancel Culture as a spreading madness, a virus of twisted thinking and immeasurable self-righteousness. There may be a patient zero somewhere who brought it into our midst, but he's not the one controlling its spread. It goes from person to person, group to group, infecting the susceptible.

It's a phenomenon made of so many types, promoted by so many institutions, and contributed to by so many sub-causes, that it's nearly impossible to know where its central powers lie or who is dictating its demands.

What is possible to know is that the infected have become the influential, acquiring and now wielding the force of academia, social media, journalism, the entertainment industry, public rioting, corporate influence, and political leadership in their quest to bring citizens in line. These days the wrong words in public can get you sued or fired or worse; the wrong words in private can terminate a once-solid relationship.

That's always been true, of course. What's changed is what constitutes "the wrong words." Historically, they have been obscenities, threats, or insults of the crudest sort. Today they include traditional beliefs about life, family, and country that until recently have been shared and respected. They can also include verbal refusals to accept the Cancel Culture's statement of faith.

That's why today's conservative may well become tomorrow's criminal, since legal retribution for unacceptable views, already a reality in some countries, seems inevitable—perhaps not now, but soon enough.

The church is not exempt. In fact, it's targeted. The freedom to promote and practice traditional biblical principles, even among ourselves, is being cancelled. The powers that courted, took over, and now utilize the force of our culture's main platforms of influence are training their sights on believers, carrying the full weight of the institutions they've converted, and saying to all of us, "It's your turn. Convert with the others or be silenced."

Same song, second verse. In the Gospels and the book of Acts, forces in the culture opposed basic Christian doctrine and used the force of culture (mobs, slander) to silence the church. When that didn't work, they turned to Rome, just as the forces of Cancel Culture are turning to government.

If you haven't gotten the memo yet, sit tight. It'll come.

OF CONTEMPT, CODES, AND COERCION

The year 2019 was the last year of the trickles—streams coming through cracks in the dam before it burst. It's not a liberal flood we're facing, nor is it just pro-gay, feminist, woke, or progressive. It's nothing short of a demand for a comprehensive overhaul of our most basic rights and assumptions, plus a uniform obedience to the new articles of faith.

The signs were already there when I felt the sting. Indeed, by July of 2019, anyone concerned about freedom of speech or civil discourse was feeling uneasy.

By then, belonging to the wrong president's cabinet could get you kicked out of a restaurant by its owner[6] and targeted by a renowned congresswoman who called for you to be publicly harassed wherever you went.[7] If you were a teenaged peaceful pro-life demonstrator, a state representative could videotape you, insult you, then suggest online that your home address and personal information should be made public.[8] If someone objected to his aggressions he would respond, "Bring it, Bible Bullies! You are bigots, sexists, and misogynists and I see right through your fake morals and your broken values."[9] Antifa, which by then could take credit for numerous documented assaults against anyone they labeled fascists, enjoyed open support from many respected leaders, including at least one congressman and a national committee chairman.[10] A presidential hopeful called for the revocation of tax-exempt status from any American church that did not affirm gay marriage.[11] Major universities had become ground zero for rioting when conservative guest speakers dared to enter their territory.[12] Christian leaders and celebrities either timidly demurred when asked their position on sexuality[13] or suffered a swift professional and societal backlash if they expressed the biblical view.[14]

That was the prelude, a season of contempt, virtue-signaling, and ever-changing guidelines for acceptable speech. But it will be remembered as the year of gloves-off, blatant, brass-knuckle combat. To my thinking, that's the year we were officially served notice.

COVID didn't help, but the year's madness was only enhanced by the virus, not created by it. Even the George Floyd tragedy[15] can't be blamed for it. Floyd's death was a green light, not a cause. It said "Charge!" to the worst elements of Cancel Culture, giving them excuse and permission to vent their hearts out. Vent they did, throwing a lethal national fit, and rewriting all our rules and assumptions about democracy and coexistence. (A much fuller discussion of the Floyd case and its aftermath will come in chapter 8.)

We saw the alleged protests over Floyd devolve into vandalism and assaults. We saw American cities taken hostage with full permission of mayors who, unfathomably, showed concern for the violators who invaded them and indifference towards the violated residents who had to endure.[16] We saw restaurant patrons terrorized,[17] freeways blocked,[18] motorists dragged from their cars for a beating,[19] and elderly pedestrians abused and threatened[20] all in the name of the new justice.

The lasting horror of 2020, though, may not be the incidents themselves, but the institutional approval—unprecedented, like everything else that year—bestowed by academics, politicians, celebrities, and influencers. The message their friendly nod to the terrorists gave was chillingly clear: if you're on the wrong side of this new wave, then powerful segments of your culture who you'd think would come to your defense will not.

An astonishingly high number of elected lawmakers ignored or minimized the injustice.[21] Journalists interpreted arson and looting as "mostly peaceful protests."[22] Over a thousand doctors and medical caregivers released an open statement admonishing all of us to stay home and socially distance unless, of course, we were out protesting, in which case the justice of our cause outweighed the health concerns the rest of the public had to take seriously.[23] Even the Speaker of the House, when questioned about destruction of public property, dismissed rational concerns with a shrug, saying, "I don't care about statues...people will do what they do."[24]

Small wonder, then, that the Cancel Culture felt emboldened to pursue their scorched-earth policy. For the first time in recent memory, anarchy not only existed, but it thrived with the consent of mainstream leaders and influencers who should have roundly condemned it.

But while anarchy thrived in the streets, tyranny seized the day on the Web. There are few sources more influential, or more utilized by Cancel Culture, than social media. There are also few experiences more frustrating than being the target of censorship from social media outlets who shut you down at whim, refuse to explain why, then insist their unexplained actions are warranted because...well, you just have to trust them, they know best.

Facebook, Twitter, and YouTube are today's ubiquitous hall monitors sending Christians and conservatives into detention with no more explanation than the "because we said so" that I got from Amazon. "I just got out of Facebook jail!" is a common online quip among believers who've posted something Big Brother found unacceptable, had their post removed or their page suspended, served their time, then were granted release with a Christ-like admonition to "Go and violate community standards no more." Arrogance has never seemed so holy, nor been so technologically advanced.

In that sense, the biggest names in social media have given us an easy-to-follow roadmap of Cancel Culture's mentality: "We define, we decide, we needn't explain."

Major social media platforms have decided they know what's true, what's moral, and what's bigoted. Based on that knowledge, they define truth, morality, and bigotry, and thereby decide who should be allowed to speak, who should be silenced, who should be scrutinized whenever they post, and whose content and messaging should be given an unexamined green light.

They know so much. Problem is, they won't deign to explain how they know, what measures they use to judge, or why Group A is allowed to share content that is clearly violent, threatening, or obscene, while Group B is forbidden to share content which contains no violence, threats, or obscenity, yet is considered (by those who know, of course) capable of making someone feel insulted or unsafe.

Social media bias is astonishing, even to those of us who've been accustomed to media bias for decades. Conservative individuals or groups, some of them very prominent and credible, are having their content removed, suspended, or demonetized with no pretense of an explanation.

A quick search of the Internet shows, for example, the apologetics site PragerU had videos pulled or restricted because they were deemed "inappropriate for younger audiences." Those offending videos included one by Harvard University law professor Alan Dershowitz on the founding of Israel, and other such "inappropriate for children" titles as "Why America Must Lead," "The Ten Commandments: Do Not Murder," and "Why Did America Fight the Korean War."[25]

CBN's Chris Mitchell's prayer for Israel was likewise (and laughingly) deemed "age inappropriate."[26] and staff members of Twitter admitted, on hidden camera, to censoring conservatives by "shadow banning" them, limiting their content visibility.[27] The Media Research Center (MRC) conducted a study finding that Facebook, along with Twitter, YouTube, and Google, relies on the left-wing Southern Poverty Law Center (SPLC) to identify "hate" groups and then suppress or remove them from its platform. According to the report, "Over time, Facebook deleted the pages of at least 57 groups at the behest of the SPLC."[28]

Three separate studies confirmed that search engine results on Google "favored liberal sites or liberal candidates," and after Google engineer James Damore wrote an internal memo criticizing the company's "Ideological Echo Chamber," he was fired.[29]

The online censoring of social or theological conservatives is too widespread and overwhelming to give adequate space to in this chapter, and in fact, the topic could easily become a book of its own.

That's the sad fact that led MRC President Bozell to confirm: "Voices are being silenced, opinions are being censored and conservative media are being suppressed. These tech companies claim they provide platforms to connect people and share ideas. However, when the only ideas permitted are from one side, any prospect of intellectual discourse dies."[30]

NOTICE IS HEREBY SERVED

Publicly overpower another person or group, and you serve notice to other persons and groups: "Surrender or suffer." That's why the virus of Cancel Culture is so relevant to you and me, and that's how its impact is being felt by believers.

An interesting verse from 1 Timothy 5:20 advises, "Those who are sinning rebuke in the presence of all, that the rest also may fear." Paul knew that when a person gets nailed in front of others, then the others, fearing the same fate, will avoid whatever offense got that person nailed. Public rebuke inspires public fear.

That's redemptive if done for the right reason, in the right way. But the approach has its dark side, as shown in the results of the kind of bullying described earlier. When people are abused in public, other people, fearing the same fate, will try to avoid displeasing the abuser. Millions of Americans saw the public assaults and humiliations imposed by Cancel Culture activists. Too many of those millions, Christians included, have been subdued, afraid to speak their minds in front of today's bellowing, building-burning Goliaths. Author Ed Abbey pointed this out when he noted: "The one thing…that is truly ugly is the climate of hate and intimidation, created by a noisy few, which makes the decent majority reluctant to air in public their views on anything controversial…Where all pretend to be thinking alike, it's likely that no one is thinking at all."[31]

It's a classic trickle-down effect. On the one hand, it trickles down to people who hold the views of the intimidator by empowering them to not only express their beliefs but to also trample on those who don't. So the feminist who already takes a pro-choice view feels all the more encouraged to denigrate those who don't when she sees them denigrated publicly by an elected official.[32] The "woke" university student already contemptuous of his parents' belief in the Bible feels encouraged to dismiss them entirely when he sees talk show hosts do the same.[33] When activists call for a church to be burned down while a local elected leader calls for its pastor to be deported, all because of the pastor's objection to a gay pride celebration,[34] then anyone holding a pro-gay view is encouraged to attack everyone else who doesn't.

On the other hand, it trickles down in a very different way to those holding the beliefs Cancel Culture wants cancelled. The "decent majority reluctant to air their views," cited by Abbey, has a pretty good idea what those forbidden views are: "binary" views of the two sexes as being inborn and distinct, "homophobic" views that marriage is heterosexual in nature, "racist" views that racism is determined by words and actions rather than race, "sexist" views that the unborn deserve to become the born, and "fundamentalist" views that hell exists, man is sinful, and God can be known only through His Son Jesus.

When the voices surrounding you say you're wrong, you might be tempted to reconsider your beliefs, especially if you never really examined and became grounded in them in the first place. That's when you might think, *Well, how can so many people be wrong? Maybe there's something to what they say.*

That's exactly why I think a number of not-too-well-grounded Christians have waffled on key issues. They believed the right things but only because they occasionally heard them mentioned by pastors. Not being students of Scripture themselves, they never studied their positions or thought them through. If they were grounded more on the sand than the rock (Matthew 7:24-27), then it's no wonder they were susceptible to worldly wisdom.

That may be why some of your Christian friends are caving to the Cancel Culture.

But even if you are sure of your beliefs that doesn't mean you're willing to declare them. The trickle-down effect of cultural bullying can be the conversion of the unlearned, but it can also be the intimidation of the learned. Ungrounded Christians won't be able to stand; grounded but intimidated Christians won't be willing to.

That may be why you're tempted to cave to the Cancel Culture.

HOME IS WHERE THE HEARTBREAK IS

Refusing to bend is one thing when the risk is society's disapproval. It becomes something else, something personal and profound, when the risk is a relationship with someone who's deeply loved.

Just ask the parents of kids who cut them off because they voted for the wrong candidate. Or hold the wrong views on sexuality. Or won't admit they're racist.

One of the cruelest symptoms of the Cancel Culture virus is the implacability the infected show towards their bewildered loved ones. It's a new form of shunning, that quaint practice of cutting off all ties with the excommunicated.

It's worse, in fact. At least in the practice of shunning, cold as it is, the social rejection is imposed on backsliders who strayed from beliefs they once shared with their community. The community feels betrayed and indignant, so they shun. But Cancel Culture doesn't punish friends and loved ones for turning away from beliefs they used to share. Instead, it shuns them for *not* turning towards beliefs the shunner now holds. "My enlightenment opened my eyes to your wickedness," he says. "You must now turn from it, or I'll turn from you."

The old liberal ideas—tolerance, diversity, coexistence—are now, themselves, intolerable. A running theme you'll hear from universities, activist groups such as Antifa and Black Lives Matter, and folks who are "woke," is that there's no room for "agreeing to disagree" over the views they've decided are unacceptable. The new views are the only legitimate ones, so keeping company with those holding on to the old views is seen as a moral compromise.

The tears and pleas of heartbroken families and friends go unheeded. Parents may ask, "Can't we love each other despite our differences?" Friends may say, "Let's just drop these subjects and get along." But this social reform is also a societal purge, where arguments for diversity are seen as attempts to continue in heresy. Its goal of purity can't be realized if true believers intermingle with heretics, so no, relations with the unenlightened are as forbidden as intermarriage between ancient Israel and the Canaanites.

Cancel Culture zealots value purity above all, even above fair treatment of others or relations with people they used to love. Screenwriters Warren Beatty and Trevor Griffiths described this ruthlessness pretty well in their 1981 film *Reds* when a character defended the Socialist takeover in Russia:

> "What did you think this thing was gonna be? A revolution by consensus where we all sat down and agreed over a cup of coffee? Did you really expect social transformation to be anything other than a murderous process? It's a war, E.G., and we gotta fight it like we fight a war, with discipline, with terror, with firing squads, or we just give it up."[35]

We've seen the discipline in the Cancel Culture's commitment to purity. We've seen the terror in its rioting, vandalism, and assault. It remains to be seen whether the firing squads will arrive and what form they will take when they do.

SPEAK NOW OR FOREVER REGRET HOLDING YOUR PEACE

The silence of the lambs isn't just a movie title. It's today's sad reality, the result of those infected with the Cancel Culture virus influencing some Christian sheep who ignore ancient principles God has laid down clearly and firmly:

1. Do not take moral or spiritual instructions from the surrounding world.

2. Do not adjust the moral and spiritual instructions I've given you to those of the surrounding world.

3. Do not let the surrounding world keep you from living and teaching the moral and spiritual instructions I've given you.

Israel got that very memo, a clear warning to avoid undue influence from the surrounding nations: "According to the doings of the land of Egypt, where you dwelt, you shall not do; and according to the doings of the land of Canaan, where I am bringing you, you shall not do; *nor shall you walk in their ordinances*" (Leviticus 18:3, emphasis mine).

The Hebrew word translated "ordinance" is *chuqqah,* meaning "statute, ordinance, limit, enactment, customs, something prescribed." God was saying, in essence, "Don't be like them, and don't be instructed by them." So said David, reaffirming this when he wrote:

> Blessed is the man
> Who walks not in the counsel of the ungodly.
> (Psalm 1:1)

It's noteworthy that Jesus reminded His followers that "If the world hates you, you know that it hated Me before it hated you" (John 15:18). He also warned that opposition from the culture is no excuse for timidity: "For whoever is ashamed of Me *and My words* in this adulterous and sinful generation, of him the Son of Man also will be ashamed when He comes in the glory of His Father with the holy angels" (Mark 8:38, emphasis mine).

We've been served notice. The notice says that some of His words are unacceptable in today's marketplace of ideas. Some of us are thereby avoiding that marketplace altogether or backing down once we get there. Both responses show the trickle-down effects of the Cancel Culture's intimidation tactics.

Those effects include the poisoned air we're seeing between friends, loved ones, colleagues, church members, and citizens. The Cancel Culture has brought with it mistrust and fear, fueling the temptation to just start saying the right things in order to appease or to stop saying anything in order to avoid.

But we're given neither the option of refashioning nor omitting our Creator's words just to appease a hostile culture or to placate hostile loved ones. Loving others as God so loved the world when He sent Christ includes showing them respect and consideration, trying to preserve relations with them, serving them with good works, and speaking truth to them as opportunity and wisdom allow.

But it never means letting them tell us what to believe, practice, or say. They are loved, but they are not Lord.

CHAPTER FOUR

YOU'VE BEEN STARRED

The Cancel Culture has served notice to us, but it's served something else to the general public. It's served them a portrait of us, painted without our consent. Presented as an accurate portrayal, it is, in fact, a caricature, like the distorted image you see when looking into a funhouse mirror. I call it "starring," a process we should understand better if we want to communicate well with folks who think that distorted image is the real us.

When Australian pastor Josh Williamson heard that an activist named Stephen Hick had called on local businesses to refuse serving anyone from Williamson's church because of his views on sexuality, he wryly asked, "I am not sure how Mr. Hick is going to identify those connected with our church, perhaps he'll want us to wear a yellow cross on our shirts?"[1]

He was referring, of course, to the yellow stars Jewish citizens had to wear under the Nazi regime. The history of "starring" is worth remembering because it's a template for understanding patterns we see in ancient history, modern history, and current events.

Starring is a derivative of the "misrepresent, then mistreat" tactic. We see it in the Gospels, when Jesus was attacked and killed because people misrepresented Him, repeating things He never said or distorting things He actually did say. In so doing, they created a monster who had to be destroyed.

He said people would destroy the temple of His body and in three days He would raise it up (John 2:19). They misquoted Him by saying He threatened to destroy the temple in Jerusalem (Matthew 26:61). He said render to Caesar what Caesar was due and to God what He was due (Matthew 22:21). They misquoted Him by saying He told His followers not to pay taxes (Luke 23:2). He said His kingdom was not of this world (John 18:36). They misrepresented Him by saying He stirred up and perverted the nation (Luke 23:2,5).

They wanted Him silenced. They also knew they couldn't get people to act against Him based on His *actual* words, so they got people to act against Him based on a *distortion* of His words. Misrepresentation is a critical part of starring, and it's scary to see how far that tactic can get you.

It got Hitler awfully far when his propogandists began "educating" the German people on the danger Jews posed. First it had to be shown that Jews were both malignant and powerful. That way, when they were persecuted, it would look like the former bullies were simply getting what they deserved.

So the Nazi propaganda machine persuaded Germans that the Jews "dominated the economic and political life of Germany," that they were "rich and clever," and that Hitler's struggle was against their "menace."[2] A susceptible public became convinced that Germany's well-being was threatened by Jews, not because of who they really were but because of how they were misrepresented.

Once that stereotype of "the Jew" was commonly accepted, mistreatment became easier. After they'd been maligned, they were "starred," publicly identified, and deprived of rights others had because they were, after all, "those people." Convince society that a group is lethal, and few in that society will object when you strip away that group's rights.

Holocaust survivor Corrie ten Boom described this in her autobiography *The Hiding Place:* "The true horror of occupation came over us only slowly. A rock through the window of a Jewish owned store. An ugly word scrawled on the wall of a Synagogue. It was as though they were trying us, testing the temper of the country. How many Dutchmen would go along with them? And the answer, to our shame, was many."[3]

That's the power of starring, similar to what's seen today when people are convinced of the worst anti-Christian myths and stereotypes. Our beliefs are neither dangerous nor hateful, but they do conflict with the agendas of some and the consciences of others who do what the Pharisees and the Nazis did: they mispresent, presenting their misrepresentations as fact, influencing who they can.

We believe, for example, that God creates people as male or female, a status that cannot be changed and should be embraced. Those demanding a complete affirmation of transgenderism dislike that belief, but the belief itself isn't striking enough to whip people up against us. So they take it a step further by saying we not only disapprove of sex-reassignment attempts, but that we also hate transgender persons, or are transphobic, so we encourage people to hate them, while encouraging them to hate themselves.

We also believe people are responsible before God for their own sins, not the sins of people who lived before them. Those demanding a uniform belief in the racism and guilt of all white people realize our belief is not enough to create a reaction. But interpreting that belief as evidence of racism, then lumping the alleged racists in with groups like the KKK, can spark a literal riot.

We believe there is only one way to God through His Son Jesus. Those demanding a more "progressive" spirituality realize our belief is not dangerous, however strongly they may reject it. But they still don't like it. So comparing us to madmen who flew airplanes into American buildings on 9/11 because they believed there was only one way, or with the torturers of the Inquisition who believed there was only one way, they can turn public opinion against us. Not because of what we really believe but because of the mythical hatred they link with our belief.

That leaves us facing a systematic hostility, directed not toward all self-identified Christians but toward those believing and teaching biblical essentials, especially the doctrines we're discussing here. *Star-ring* and *hostility* are fair words to use.

So is another word we should use sparingly, but still use when it fits: *persecution.*

WHEN THE SHOE FITS

Persecution doesn't apply to every pushback we get. If someone disagrees with us, we're not being persecuted. Nor is it persecution if someone openly criticizes us, corrects us, or scrutinizes our words. It's self-serving to claim victimhood whenever we're challenged, and just as surely as we have a right to speak, others have the right to critique what we say and how we say it.

I'd even say mockery, in most cases, doesn't qualify for the *p* word. We might be called crazy and not like it, but it hardly injures us. Nor do stand-up comedians who make jokes at our expense, TV shows who satire us, or the many forms of communication that have made Christians look like buffoons. I can remember a left-wing Northern California journalist writing that I resembled "an aging member of the Village People singing group," and in Southern California, the *OC Weekly* listed me in 2004 as one of Orange county's "50 Scariest People."

That might be irritating (the Village People?) but it's sure not the rack.

The Greek word translated as "persecution" in the New Testament bespeaks something stronger. *Diōgmos* means, per *Strong's Concordance*, to "pursue someone with hostility, or to harass, oppress, molest, trouble, or bring judgment onto another person." So whenever a person or group is subject to harassment, hostile pursuit, or oppression (the exercise of harsh control over another, also per *Strong's*), then persecution is happening.

It happens to different degrees, sometimes to the point of torture and death, as experienced by Christians in North Korea, Afghanistan, or Somalia.[4] That's the level of mistreatment we usually think of when using the term, calling to mind the arrests, imprisonments, and executions of believers recorded in the book of Acts, *Foxe's Book of Martyrs*, and endless other accounts of past and current persecutions.

But just as the word shouldn't be wrongly applied, it also shouldn't be wrongly avoided. If Party A targets and pursues Party B with hostility, interfering unjustly with Party B's ability to speak or function ("harassing," "troubling," "bringing judgment onto," "imposing harsh control"), then Party A, be it Cancel Culture, government, or individual, is a persecutor, and Party B is the persecuted. A headache needn't be a migraine in order to qualify as a headache, and persecution needn't include prison and death in order to qualify as persecution.

Just as levels of persecution vary from country to country, so do the kind of words or actions triggering it. In nations that are under rigid Islamic or Communist rule, just being identified as Christian is enough to land you in prison, or worse.

But in America, Canada, and a number of Latin and European countries, it's not so simple. In those regions, only certain Christian teachings will get you in trouble. Hold to those teachings, and you'll get starred.

Remember, misrepresentation comes before mistreatment. So by the time Jews in Germany had to wear the yellow star, the German population had been taught to believe the worst about them. When they saw the star, to them it didn't just mean Jew. It also meant evil, Marxist, Socialist, white slave trafficker, and the source of most other national maladies.[5] With that distortion embedded, the misrepresented could now become the mistreated.

The German government began denying Jews membership in medical school or participation in the medical or legal profession.[6] Jewish civilian workers were fired from the army, and Jewish officers were expelled.[7] Jews were then forbidden to slaughter animals according to purity rituals for Kosher meals, thus preventing them from being able to practice basic aspects of their faith.[8] Brownshirts publicly destroyed Jewish shops and properties, to the applause of too many German citizens.[9] Books challenging any of the tenets of the Third Reich were deemed intolerable and fit for burning.[10] Then came the laws against their participation in all aspects of public life, then the Jewish ghettos, then the camps, then the Final Solution. But it all began with a distortion.

We are hardly Jews under Nazi abuse, and the Holocaust shouldn't be used casually by anyone feeling mistreated. Still, some parallels are hard to miss.

Students who attended Christian universities are now hindered from attending law school because they graduated from an institution holding the wrong beliefs about sex and family.[11] Medical students objecting to abortion, or claiming their Christian faith as a guiding principle, can experience similar "viewpoint discrimination."[12] Christian universities holding the traditional views about homosexuality and transgenderism are now in danger of having their accreditations stripped.[13] A military chaplain lost his job and his pension over a sermon in which he said all sexual sins, whether heterosexual or homosexual, were equally wrong.[14] Christian pastors and counselors are being forbidden to apply the biblical definition of marriage and sexual sin, thus preventing them from being able to practice basic aspects of their faith.[15] Activists have threatened to tear down pictures, statues, or stained-glass windows portraying a "White Jesus."[16] Groups such as Antifa and Black Lives Matter publicly destroy shops and property, and have openly threatened to also target churches, again, as before, to the applause of too many citizens.[17] Books challenging the tenets of Cancel Culture are deemed intolerable and are being banned.[18]

When the Pennsylvania lawmaker described earlier called pro-lifers "Bible bullies, bigots, sexists, and misogynists" holding "fake morals and broken values,"[19] he did some classic starring. Having categorized them as deplorables, he could justify the abuse he heaped on them. No wonder, at another location, a young California thug, also mentioned earlier, felt free to punch out an elderly man holding a pro-life sign.[20] If a growing number of people see their anti-abortion neighbors as contemptible, then why shouldn't they act on their contempt?

Convince the public someone is evil, and the public will offer little resistance when you malign, then limit, then assault that someone. It's a dynamic found in the ancient history of the Gospels, the modern history of the Holocaust, and the heavy-handedness of today's Cancel Culture.

"YOU KNOW ME BETTER THAN THAT!"

Against that backdrop, it's tragic but not surprising when someone you've cherished suddenly attaches the bigot star onto your jacket. If leaders within government, academia, psychiatry, and media all say you should wear it, then someone who should know better just might believe them.

Especially if they hold views you disapprove of or if they're living outside the bounds of what they know you believe. That's why the daughter raised in a Christian home who chooses to live with her boyfriend will be susceptible to voices telling her that Mom and Dad are judgmental and hurtful. The son of believing parents who identifies as a woman will be tempted to believe the elites who assure him that he's the offspring of "toxic transphobics." The sister who had an abortion may likewise prefer calling her pro-life brother a sexist, as many in the culture now do.

You might protest, "But you know me better than that!" True, but look at it through the eyes of that daughter, son, or sister. They want to believe they're right, and in many cases, they're not entirely sure they are. So if Christian loved ones disagree with them, and the Cancel Culture labels that disagreement as hatred, then starring those friends or family members makes it easier to dismiss their positions.

Just as susceptible are those wanting to be, or priding themselves on already being, "enlightened." Someone who objects to your views may never have had an abortion, felt attracted to the same sex, or experienced gender identity confusion. But in their social and professional circles, they may see Christian morality as something that intellectually evolved people dismiss. For the sake of maintaining their enlightened status, they may feel the need to dismiss you too.

It's not fair, and as you may already know, it's very, very hurtful. But the hard reality of it has to be faced.

YOUR STARRING ROLE

If you're holding the wrong views, there are people who want businesses to refuse you, social media to censor you, retailers to ban your product, crowds to shout you down when you speak, professions to bar you, and corporations to fire you. That's just for starters.

We ignore history's lessons to our peril, and what does history show us, if not that the unthinkable today is the *Six O'Clock News* tomorrow? Be honest. If someone told you in 2017 that in the America of 2020, you would witness unrestrained mob riots, city takeovers, vandalism, and group assaults on both police and citizens, along with the widespread permission of this madness from officials in high places, would you have believed them?

That's my point. I really don't think we're on the road to execution. Still, when a growing segment of our own culture considers us dangerous or loathsome or both, as Nazis considered Jews to be, then let's be realistic. The extreme wing of any group represents its endgame. So the extreme wing of the Cancel Culture—be it Antifa, the BLM movement, or individual extremists—has proven through its public assaults that it considers violence an acceptable, even necessary option.

True, most of their colleagues would disapprove, at least for now. Then again, in the late thirties, Hitler's propaganda machine could hardly say, "We hate Jews, so we're building death camps for them." The public wouldn't have cooperated. Instead, it acclimated the public year by year, step by step, removing layer after layer of their Jewish neighbors' humanity, until the indoctrinated public became the indifferent public, turning away with a shrug as their fellow citizens were finally carted off.

We the starred are in danger. It's a leap to assume the danger is a literal death penalty, but it's naïve to assume it's not severe.

So do we now cry "martyrdom" and feel sorry for ourselves? God forbid. Looking realistically at a situation helps us prepare for it, instead of running from it or letting it catch us unawares. "See then that you walk circumspectly," Paul said, "not as fools but as wise, redeeming the time, because the days are evil" (Ephesians 5:15-16). To walk circumspectly means to walk with awareness, a clear direction, and a refusal to be fazed by obstacles, even when the days are evil.

The alternative is to let the Cancel Culture overwhelm us, intimidate us, distract us, or get us so riled up in frustration that we lose direction and perspective.

Jesus modeled a better way, one of balance. He never lost focus of His mission to seek and save the lost (Matthew 18:11), but was fully aware of who His adversaries were (John 5:42), what games they were trying to play (Matthew 22:18), how unreasonable they were (Matthew 11:16-19), and why they hated His message (John 3:19-21).

REPROACH AND REWARD

He bore *reproach* in this world (Romans 15:3) while remembering the *reward* of the next (Hebrews 12:2). To His followers today, I think He'd repeat what He told His followers before: *Go and do likewise.*

To bear reproach is to be reviled, and Paul explained why reproach is part of a disciple's life: "For to this end we both labor and suffer reproach, because we trust in the living God, who is the Savior of all men, especially of those who believe" (1 Timothy 4:10).

To trust in the living God is to obey Him, since faith without works is dead (James 2:26). Obeying Him means fulfilling His commission to preach the gospel and make disciples (Matthew 28:19-20; Mark 16:15). To make disciples is to teach them so they in turn will teach others (2 Timothy 2:2), and to teach is to give the full counsel of God from the Word of God in its entirety (Acts 20:27; 2 Timothy 3:16). That will include teaching what the Word says about sex, marriage, preborn life, prejudice, salvation, and judgment. That, in turn, will lead to reproach.

Nothing new about that. In stark contrast to our natural desire to be liked, Jesus calls us not to be deliberately disliked but to be prepared if and when we are: "If the world hates you, you know that it hated Me before it hated you. If you were of the world, the world would love its own. Yet because you are not of the world, but I chose you out of the world, therefore the world hates you" (John 15:18-19).

What is the primary reason the world hated Jesus? His words. What He said infuriated all the wrong people, who conspired to kill Him because they knew words have influence, and the influence of His words on the people would disrupt their agenda and control. Both He and His words had to be stopped.

It happened to Him; it happens to us. Paul elaborated on that when he told the Corinthians: "Being reviled, we bless; being persecuted, we endure; being defamed, we entreat. We have been made as the filth of the world, the offscouring of all things until now" (1 Corinthians 4:12-13).

The message bearer bears the reproach of the message, a point nicely underscored in Hebrews: "Therefore let us go forth to Him, outside the camp, bearing His reproach" (Hebrews 13:13). That reproach is a badge of honor, a judgment against those who threw it on us assuming it dishonored us, not knowing that, in fact, it dishonors them: "And not in any way terrified by your adversaries, which is to them a proof of perdition, but to you of salvation" (Philippians 1:28).

When truth is told, reproach follows, but that's not all, thank God. Truth also yields life, so when the Word is sown, it falls on bad ground yielding thorns and good ground bringing fruit (Matthew 13:1-23). There's the beauty and the adventure in ministering the Word of God— reproach and rejoicing.

Still, who likes reproach? As citizens we hope to live and speak freely, uninterrupted by laws or movements trying to silence us. We also hope our words, not distortions of them, are what people will hear when we speak.

Those hopes aren't always realized. Too often we're reproached in ways that are hateful or humiliating. I prefer being hated. When we're hated, we feel the isolation and we may suffer any number of consequences. But when we're humiliated, we endure one of our worst fears. We're mocked and shamed, standing before a jeering crowd as vulnerable as a junior high student surrounded by mimicking bullies. In that vulnerability, all dignity is stripped from us and we're left feeling defenseless.

So was He. I've seen Golgotha, where it all happened, and it's awful to realize He hung there naked within spitting distance of His mockers. I've spent most of my adult life trying to achieve and maintain a level of personal dignity and professional respect, yet this naked suffering Messiah is the One who calls me to follow Him, right into His willingness to be humiliated for the sake of the truth.

That's reproach. To bear it, we'll need some real inspiration, and that's where reward comes in.

"Let this mind be in you," Paul wrote, "which was also in Christ

Jesus" (Philippians 2:5). He then explains how Christ bore the cross knowing what would happen: "Therefore God also has highly exalted Him and given Him the name which is above every name" (Philippians 2:9). The reward for the reproach was worth it.

The author of Hebrews advises us to do the same, providing a terrific reason for going outside the camp to bear His reproach: "For here we have no continuing city, but we seek the one to come" (Hebrews 13:14).

There it is, a truth we need to land on, meditate over, and absorb deeply. This life is not it! We are running a race for which we'll be rewarded, on a day of reckoning when we stand like athletes before the Judge: "For we must all appear before the judgment seat of Christ, that each one may receive the things done in the body, according to what he has done, whether good or bad" (2 Corinthians 5:10).

If I apply my thoughts toward the date I have with the judgment seat, where I'll be rewarded for stewarding truth no matter how well or how poorly it was received, then I feel pumped to continue bearing the reproach.

For the Cancel Culture, the battle is temporal. They want a new world down here, at any cost. But as much as we want this world to be at its best, we know it will pass away and that our citizenship is elsewhere (Philippians 3:20). So we speak the truth about basic doctrines, first to faithfully represent God, second for the sake of those who will hear and respond, and third, as a judgment on those who hear and reject, leaving them without excuse.

With that eternal perspective on reproach and reward, we can accept that whatever comes of speaking the truth, it will come because we, by God's grace, said yes to the mandate of being not just believers, but also expressers and practitioners of our beliefs. It's the doers of God's Word, not just those giving it lip service, who get the pushback.

Shadrach, Meshach, and Abed-Nego were thrown into a furnace not just for believing in God but for refusing to bow to an idol because of that belief (Daniel 3:1-18).

Daniel was thrown into a lions' den not just for being a Hebrew, but for defying the order to pray to a man because he prayed only to the God of Abraham, Isaac, and Jacob (Daniel 6:7-17).

John the Baptist was beheaded not just for believing in the Messiah, but for speaking the truth about Herod's sexual immorality, as a follower of God and the Messiah He sent (Matthew 14:3-4).

Sir Thomas More was executed not just for his faith but for his unwillingness to recognize a marriage that was not sanctioned by God, an unwillingness emboldened by his faith.

Christian abolitionists ran afoul of the law not just because of their Christianity, but because of their commitment, as those the Son had set free, to bringing slaves to freedom.

Corrie ten Boom was sent to a concentration camp not just for believing in Christ, but for sheltering Jews at her own peril out of love for her Lord's chosen people.

In all cases, people of faith suffered because faith produced love for truth, and love for truth demanded its expression in words and actions. Great rewards followed great reproach.

The Jews of World War II had their stars cruelly imposed on them against their will, dooming them. For this we have to weep with deep respect for levels of suffering we'll never know.

But we, when we're starred, experience something very different. We have a choice, making us willing recipients of the reproach, fully aware that whatever difficulties come from being starred can be avoided if only we'll yield. Yet we say no to yielding and yes to the outcome, be it personal heartache, social rejection, professional hardship, or criminal status. We're all in, and we'll stay all in so long as we value eternal truth over temporal convenience.

Today the voice of Cancel Culture says, "Shut up." Soon the voice governing the Uncancelled Kingdom will say, "Well done." Our decision's a no-brainer. We'll tolerate the one for now, so we can enjoy the other forever.

CHAPTER FIVE

WHY THE HOSTILITY?

We may understand what starring is, yet still wonder *why* it is. What could move people to either create or accept such a negative view of us?

A virus like Cancel Culture needs someone to infect, and those with an already weakened immune system will be its first targets. Which raises the question of the infected: who are they, and what made them susceptible?

You may have asked that while watching interviews with accomplished, professional adults who go absolutely off the rails when commenting on people like you. You may have heard acidic remarks made about you by celebrities, journalists, or politicians, remarks so insulting you know they'd never make them about any other group. Or maybe someone you've known and enjoyed a good relationship with has turned against you, deciding you're no longer a fit companion.

It can be downright weird, like a horror film where people taken over by aliens look and sound the same, but suddenly aren't. In real life, as in the movie, people are left scratching their heads, saying, "What the heck happened?"

I've felt for some time now that some combination of these three elements contribute to Cancel Culture: convenience, conscience, and conviction.

CONVENIENCE ("COULD YOU MOVE YOUR WORDS, PLEASE? THEY'RE IN MY WAY")

Whenever truth is told, someone is inconvenienced.

Paul saw this firsthand when he preached in Ephesus and got a widespread response, with former worshippers of the goddess Diana turning to the true God (Acts 19:1-20). That hardly set well with Demetrius, the local silversmith who made good money fashioning and selling shrines to Diana. Seeing that the gospel was bad for business, he corralled other shrine-makers to join him in whipping up a riot against Paul (Acts 19:23-29), whose words were getting in the way.

Elijah's words proved inconvenient to Ahab when he rebuked the king for following Baal. True to form, the man inconvenienced by the truth blamed the truthteller, accusing him of "troubling Israel" when in fact, Ahab was Israel's real troubler (1 Kings 18:17-18).

Jesus' teaching likewise proved troubling to religious leaders whose authority was undermined by His words. Even if He hadn't rebuked their hypocrisy (Matthew 23:13-15) and warned that no one would get into heaven unless his righteousness exceeded theirs (Matthew 5:20), just His explanation of God's grace toward sinners (Luke 18:9-14) and of Himself as the Savior (John 3:16) dismantled the hold they wanted to retain over the people. His truth would set people free, but that freedom was a mighty inconvenience to those who neither wanted it for themselves or for others (Matthew 23:13).

As it was then, so it is today—when the gospel is preached, someone will be inconvenienced. "Someone," especially these days, can be a broad category, covering governments, political factions, or the Cancel Culture.

Governments wanting complete, unquestioning allegiance will find Christianity very inconvenient indeed. The first and great commandment requires love for God with the entire heart, soul, and mind (Matthew 22:37-38). Such a love need not exclude love for country or government, but it trumps them both, saying, as Sir Thomas More is reported to have said, "I die the King's good servant, and God's first."[1]

That will never be acceptable to the Kim family of North Korea, who demand fidelity to themselves first and foremost.[2] Nor will it fly in Islamic strongholds like Somalia, Pakistan, or Libya, among others.[3] To affirm in any of these nations that Jesus is the only way to God is to reject the culture's orthodoxy.

Whereas this defiance of government power brings jail or death in some nations, in our own America, the scenario is serious though much less severe. It can evoke another kind of persecution.

It evokes it from certain political factions and social causes, because our doctrines are an affront to their views about justice and love.

Belief in the exclusivity of Jesus is viewed as discriminatory, belief in hell is viewed as archaic, belief in man's sinfulness is viewed as self-loathing and judgmental, belief in the normalcy of the male-female sexual union is viewed as homophobic, belief in the immutable nature of our assigned sex is viewed as transphobic, and belief in the value of the unborn is viewed as misogynistic.

Considering all of that, anyone holding to these doctrines can expect heat from groups dedicated to protecting the right to abort, advancing the normalizing of transgenderism, demanding approval of homosexuality, or broadening the definition of salvation through syncretism (the attempt to mix different religions into one formula).

This puts us in the crosshairs of Planned Parenthood, the Human Rights Campaign, the Southern Poverty Law Center, the Gay and Lesbian Alliance Against Defamation (GLAAD), and the National Council of Churches, to name a few. These are hardly lightweight groups, their influence broad and strong, so when they speak to the culture, much of the culture listens and responds. When it hears from these heavy hitters that certain Christians are a danger to society, too many Americans accept the accusation without question or examination.

But it's not only certain causes or groups who'll react. Advocates for government expansion will too, often linking arms with those who are inconvenienced by these teachings, because where their causes go, big government flourishes.

With that flourishing come speech codes, broadened definitions of civil rights, and new corporate policies and requirements. Needless to say, expanded codes mean expanded violations, which require expanded enforcement, which requires expanded government. Each group scratches the others' backs pretty nicely.

Not all government expansion is wrong, and sometimes it's sorely needed. When states insisted on the right to buy and sell other human beings, government had a duty to step in, even if it provoked a civil war. If some citizens demanded the right to refuse services, jobs, and housing based on race, then government was right to intervene. When it can be verified that human rights are being trampled, then force of law rightly comes into play.

But today, human feelings being hurt are interpreted as human rights being trampled. So when an advocacy group claims, "These beliefs are causing us psychological damage," or "These beliefs inspire hatred," it becomes necessary, in the minds of the offended, to do something about it.

That's when Big Brother steps in, forming bureaucracies to investigate charges of hate speech, then imposing punishment as needed. More offices, more staff, bigger budgets, and broader state reach will follow, all of which inflate the state, making the causes and goals of the offended groups a big government dream. These groups are, after all, prone to demand enforcement of their views and redress for their grievances, solutions only an expanded government can provide. Angelo Codevilla wrote about this trend in *The American Mind*: "It invited whoever perceives himself disadvantaged or dishonored to construe himself part of such a category and to invite the government to discriminate against his foe. As government joined in some people's quarrels against others, government became fomenter and partisan in endless strife."[4]

So when the gospel is preached and biblical teachings held fast, we can now run afoul of causes, political factions, and government itself. The trending is becoming ever more clear: certain inconveniences will not be tolerated.

For those who'll embrace it, truth liberates. But it irritates, sometimes beyond measure, people whose beliefs or agendas are at odds with it.

CONSCIENCE ("TURN THAT THING DOWN!")

The voice of my conscience is reliable, delicate, and sometimes very unwanted. It's one of three daily guides we're given.

I've got to rely first and foremost on the Bible for a decision-making guide. Then there's the guidance, including the uncomfortable conviction, of the Holy Spirit. But my conscience, informed by the Scriptures and hopefully influenced by the Spirit, is also an important, God-given mechanism reminding me of what I know to be true, even if I wish it wasn't.

Conscience is referred to thirty-two times in the New Testament with the Greek word *syneidesis*, meaning "the soul as distinguishing between what is morally good and bad, prompting to do the former and shun the latter, commending one, condemning the other."

It's the mechanism by which an adulterous woman's accusers were convicted of their own sins (John 8:9), and it's implanted in all humans, Christian or non-Christian (Romans 2:15). It can be ignored, violated, or even seared to the point of becoming nonfunctional (1 Timothy 4:2), but it exists. Not allowing it to do its job is a deadly mistake.

I've made that mistake when a decision had to be made, and my conscience wanted an audience before I made it. But I wanted what my conscience didn't, so I exercised free will and decided that no, conscience won't get a vote. It objected, upping its volume rudely. I countered by covering my ears and singing *La La La*, refusing to listen, choosing to ignore. To keep my rebellion intact, I had to harden myself to that inner voice.

Then other voices would come along, sometimes through friends I ran into or a sermon I'd hear on the radio, saying audibly what my muffled conscience was trying to get across. When those voices said what I was telling my conscience to shut up about, I had to choose between listening to them or ignoring them too.

Or avoiding them. Or, in extreme cases, demonizing them. If I could make them the bad guys, then I could discount their words and stop my ears to their voices, because what they said was an uncomfortable reminder of what I was trying to ignore. I hated them for both the reminder and the discomfort.

When a verbal expression of truth echoes what a person knows but is trying not to know, that expression acts in concert with his conscience, and he has to choose: yield to truth or silence its messengers, both the internal and the external ones. If he chooses to silence the internal messenger, then the external one must also be cancelled.

No wonder Stephen's listeners went ballistic when he preached! This first martyr of the early church squared off with a council of scribes and elders who took umbrage with his words. Adding insult to injury, Stephen had neither their scholarly credentials nor their high standing. But when he expounded on the Law of Moses, which they prided themselves in knowing, and when his exposition ended with a direct indictment against their hardened hearts, they were "cut to the heart," slapping their hands over their ears and gnashing their teeth in rage (Acts 7:54).

Those claiming to be the most damaged by Christian teachings remind me of Stephen's gnashers. They're often people who once believed the same teachings they now want to obliterate. Having known the truth, they've decided to ignore it, reject it, or revise it. But too often those efforts don't quiet their deep discomfort, that inner sense that something's not right. What to do?

Shooting the messenger might work. But first, you've got to come up with a justification. You can hardly say, "Please stop. You're pointing out something I'm trying to ignore." But you can try convincing yourself that the discomfort the messenger's words cause is not due to your conscience or to your fear that he may be right. "Rather," you tell yourself, "what he's saying is a violation, an expression of bigotry, hate speech."

There! He has no right to hurt you with hate speech. For that matter, he has no right to hurt anyone else, anywhere else. His message harms you, so it must harm others, and you mustn't tolerate that. The messenger must be shot.

That's when books get banned, social network pages get taken down, and people lose jobs and reputations. The truth that pricked the conscience has now been reinterpreted as something evil; the person speaking it has now been reinterpreted as the evildoer. It happened to Stephen, Elijah, and Jesus Himself. Should we really be surprised when it happens today?

"The wicked flee," Proverbs tell us, "when no one pursues" (Proverbs 28:1). I've seen that flight countless times, when people interpret a Christian's words as being some form of assault, making him an enemy when he's only being a faithful steward.

Edgar Allan Poe described this power of a troubled conscience in his cautionary story "The Tell-Tale Heart."[5] In it, a man who's murdered his landlord and hidden his body beneath his floorboards is visited by police officers, inquiring about the missing landlord. The killer is not a suspect, and the police are only there to ask routine questions. But being convicted by his own conscience, and thereby seeing the constables as threats, the man is, as he himself admits, "dreadfully nervous."

Fleeing when no one is pursuing, as the questioning continues, he fancies that he actually hears his victim's heartbeat through the floorboards and that these officers must hear it too but are saying nothing just to torment him. In this guilt-induced madness, he finally screams out a confession, ripping up the floorboards and exposing his crime. All because of a wounded conscience.

Whenever I see people lashing out against voices echoing a truth they want to repress, I can't help but think of Stephen's hostile audience, the adulterous woman's guilty accusers, or Poe's tortured, terrified killer.

CONVICTION ("MY TRUTH IS MARCHING ON")

It would be a mistake, though, to assume that hostility toward biblical truth springs only from an inconvenienced agenda or a pricked conscience. There are also those who oppose out of deep conviction. They're true believers, thoroughly convinced that the doctrines we hold are dangerous and just as thoroughly committed to silencing us for the public good.

To be convinced and to be right are hardly the same, since we have the capacity to be fully persuaded, sometimes of truth and sometimes of the worst imaginable error.

On September 11, 2001, a band of zealots crashed airplanes into American buildings with full confidence their mass murder was God's will. They were true believers. In the summer of 1969, one man and three women followed Charles Manson's instructions to slaughter innocent people in their homes to bring about his apocalyptic vision. True believers, all of them. In the first half of the last century, Nazi Germany was fueled by true believers in the Third Reich, women and men as passionate about Hitler's mad doctrine as some martyrs are about the faith.

At a much calmer level, each political party has true believers. So does each social cause, and each faith counts them among its members. When true believers and truth go together, it's a thing of beauty. But true believers anchored to something other than truth can be wrong, misguided, even scary. Undeniably sincere too.

Saul of Tarsus was one. According to his own admission, the man "persecuted the church of God beyond measure and tried to destroy it" (Galatians 1:13) yet believed in what he did, so much so that even years later as a Christian, he could say, "Men and brethren, I have lived in all good conscience before God until this day" (Acts 23:1).

Surely he wasn't claiming that because his conscience had always been clear, his mistreatment of the church had therefore been right. But wrong as it was, it had been done at the time in good conscience before God, with full conviction, as a true believer.

These are cynical times, with people finding it nigh unto impossible to believe that someone they disagree with can be sincere. Our tendency is to figure that the political party we don't belong to or the candidate we don't support can't really believe what they say. They must be giving lip service to what they don't believe and are forever hiding ulterior motives and hypocrisies.

That underestimates the passion of the true believer. He exists and, for better or worse, is willing to make giant sacrifices for his cause. If we prejudge a man as insincere, we might expend needless energy trying to expose his insincerity when, in fact, we'd be smarter to try reasoning with him about his passionate though ill-founded views.

Or hers. While speaking at a church conference years ago, I was interrupted by a furious young woman protesting almost everything I had said. Before security could get her out, she'd screamed obscenities in my face and accused me of high crimes against humanity. My knee-jerk reaction was to write her off as a narcissistic child enjoying the adrenaline rush of a public tantrum. I'm glad, though, that I checked my cynicism long enough to detect a human behind the rhetoric.

She was fully convinced of her rightness and of my evil. It's hard not to respect that kind of passion, no matter how ridiculous you think a person's arguments may be.

So I signaled a time out with my hands and said, "OK, you think I'm a jerk? Fine. But let's talk about what matters. You say my ideas are crazy. I say they're founded in truth. So here's my challenge to you: Go home, grab a Bible, read the Gospel of John, and carefully review what Jesus said about Himself—His claims, His promises, His requirements—then ask God, whether you believe in Him or not, to show you if this is true."

A few years later I was greeted by a lovely young woman volunteering at the registration table for another conference I was speaking at. She rose, gave me big hug, and asked if I remembered her.

I didn't, until she reminded me when and how we'd met, a meeting I quickly recalled for obvious reasons. But you'd never have pegged her for the hostile disrupter I'd tried to reason with years before.

"I took your challenge because I wouldn't let you win," she explained with a smirk. "And you know what? After reading John and praying over it, I couldn't get it out of my head. I finally found a church and started attending, then started believing. So hey, I'm sorry I yelled at you!"

"I'm not," was all I could stammer, amazed and blessed.

Never underestimate the sincerity of a true believer. But let's also recognize that behind their hostility, there's also, more often than not, deep hurt.

In Charles Dickens's *A Tale of Two Cities*, French revolutionary Madame Defarge recalls witnessing her little sister's rape and her brother's death at the hands of an aristocrat. After both died, she made a vow: "That sister was my sister, that brother was my brother, those people were my people, and the summons to avenge these matters falls to me!"

The wave of vengeance marking the French revolt decades later fit that lady hand in glove. Crimes she had unjustly endured made it easy for her to justify crimes against anyone even remotely associated with the villains of her past. Her persecutor had been an aristocrat, so now all aristocrats must be persecuted.

When confronted by her own husband about how endless her thirst for blood had become, she retorted, "Tell the wind and the fire where to stop, but don't tell me."

Show me a hostile opponent of Christian doctrine and there's a good chance I can show you a gay man who heard from a televangelist, decades earlier, that AIDS was God's judgment on sexual perverts. Or a feminist who was told by her childhood pastor that she wasn't submissive enough to men and needed to stay in the kitchen, not the classroom. Or a former Christian now turned humanist whose mother was beaten bloody fifty years ago by his father, a church deacon in an isolated town, whose pastor ignored his mother's pleas and bruises, telling her to accept God's will.

Tell them their hostility's unfair, their methods un-American, their positions irrational, and don't be surprised if they reply, "Tell the wind and the fire where to stop, but don't tell me."

A SPIRITUAL BACKSTORY

So why the hostility? In the natural realm, I'd say hostility to certain truths can stem from the rage of the inconvenienced, the troubled in conscience, or the deep conviction of true believers. But I'd also say there's a spiritual backdrop to consider.

As mysterious as the book of Job is, it gives some clarity when it draws the curtain back to show us there are unseen battles behind events we experience but can't figure out, battles having to do with Satan's attempts to thwart God's plans and His people.

With that in mind, let's ask what we would do if we, like Satan, hated God, and thereby hated humanity because it was so loved by Him.

Not too hard to answer, is it? We'd kill what He gave life to. How else could we strike out at Him?

No enemy of God's, Satan included, can duke it out with Him, so we hardly expect the devil to go one-on-one with the Omnipotent. But while he can't injure God, he can strike pain in His heart, deceiving and destroying God's handiwork by preventing life three ways: by keeping it from being conceived, by terminating it before it's born, or by preventing a life that's been born from ever being born again.

Satan is about death. He deceived Eve into a decision causing immediate and eternal death, and that's still his end goal. For that reason he hates the life-giving and life-protecting doctrines that this world is also coming to hate.

You can see that hatred in current trends preventing life by distorting its natural source, the male and female identities, and the male to female union.

The sex we're born with is divinely assigned, as is the heterosexual union, having life-giving potential. To tamper with that, either by uniting members of the same sex or blurring the distinctions between the sexes, is to also prevent conception springing from normal intercourse, and the life-giving child-raising skills, unique to each sex, brought to the table by a mother and father. The very conception and subsequent nurturing of life, as both were intended, is thereby thwarted by homosexuality and gender identity confusion. Strike one.

Then, if he misses the chance to prevent conception, life's enemy would move on to prevent birth. As he reinterpreted plain truth to Eve ("You will not surely die"), so he would have us reinterpret our natural inclination to protect the unborn and replace it with arguments about choice, so what was conceived is now destroyed by abortion. Strike two.

Yet if physical birth does happen, no doubt the enemy who failed to prevent natural life will pull out all the stops to distort messages guiding a person to eternal life.

Make the path to God seem broad rather than narrow by silencing talk of Jesus as the only way, then stop man's ears to any nonsense about his sinful condition, baptize him in bitterness and lock him in unforgiveness, and mute any attention he might give to Jesus' words about grace and repeated warnings about hell. Do this, and you just might keep that earthly life you wanted to prevent from entering the eternal life your Enemy wants him to inherit.

Strike three, he's outta there.

If, as Paul told the Ephesians, this world runs "according to the prince of the power of the air, the spirit who now works in the sons of disobedience" (Ephesians 2:2), then it stands to reason that what he opposes would be opposed by the environment he influences.

That's when "Why so hostile?" becomes answerable from the unseen perspective as well as the visible one. We're on enemy turf, usurping his authority. No wonder he's mad, and no wonder people, many of whom are under his authority, are likewise mad.

But we've been given authority of our own. When Jesus promised Peter the gates of hell would not prevail against His church (Matthew 16:18), we should note that gates are preventive, meant to keep intruders out and prisoners in. They don't move; they block.

The gates of hell aren't coming after us, we're going after them, and they won't prevail when we do. Our ability to storm them is largely found in the Word we wield, confirmed by the power of the Holy Spirit to convict the hearers, impart faith and enlightenment to them, and bring them to life. Forget these basics, and you just might get overwhelmed by the pushback you're getting.

That's the backdrop of the conversations we're having these days and the tensions we're experiencing with friends and loved ones influenced by the Cancel Culture.

As we move ahead in these chapters, looking at the specific communication and relational challenges we're facing, along with the territory we're storming and the pushback we'll get, let's zero in on some choice words from that Great Commission (Matthew 28:19-20):

> *"All authority has been given to Me in heaven and on earth.*
> *Go therefore and make disciples of all the nations…and, lo, I*
> *am with you always, even to the end of the age."*

CHAPTER SIX

TEARS UNSHED

Discussing Abortion

n Lorraine Hansberry's play *A Raisin in the Sun*, a young African-American wife, worn down from years of financial and emotional struggle, learns she is pregnant with a second child, an addition she can hardly afford. When she tells her husband that she's just made a down payment toward an abortion, her mother-in-law, standing nearby, addresses her son:

> "Well—son, I'm waiting to hear you say something...Your wife say she going to destroy your child. And I'm waiting to hear you say we a people who give children life, not who destroys them—I'm waiting to see you stand up and look like your daddy and say we done give up one baby to poverty and that we ain't going to give up nary another one... I'm waiting. If you a son of mine, tell her!"[1]

That's where the contention has always been. Should the unborn life be sacrificed because of the hardship it might cause, or should the hardship be endured because of the unborn life's value?

Of course, *hardship* is quite the relative term. In Hansberry's play, the mother in question lives under daily stress, working full-time to scrape by, and the expense of a second child may put the family out on the street. There's also the hardship of a rape or incest victim, burdened with a pregnancy forced upon her in the most unimaginable way. Or the hardship of a woman who's already emotionally fragile, surviving an abusive relationship, terrified at the prospect of bringing another life into her miserable existence.

Then there's the hardship entertainer Stevie Nicks said she and the rest of us might have endured if she hadn't aborted her child: "There would have been no Fleetwood Mac."[2]

Remarks like that are unthinkable if a life already born were the subject, because only the vilest consider killing someone because of the inconvenience they might cause. But the preborn are another matter. Unseen and quite unable to protest they are routinely disposed of in the name of choice, privacy, hardship, or convenience. If they are not human, then it's no one's business. If they are human, it's everyone's.

WHERE SCIENCE AND INTUITION MEET

Intuition seems to tell us the development happening in a pregnant woman is something to protect and treasure. We're deferential in her presence, gentler, sensing without being told that she and what she's carrying warrant special care. The mere act of bumping into her is disconcerting, so how much more the idea of killing what's inside her?

I believe our natural instinct is pro-life. More than ever, science is confirming that instinct.

Contentious as the subject is, some basics are agreed on by all sides because they're inarguable. We know that when the egg is fertilized by the sperm, a zygote is formed. We also know the zygote, the first cell resulting from conception, is made of human DNA and has "a genetic composition that is absolutely unique to itself, different from any other human that has ever existed, including that of its mother (thus disproving the claim that what is involved in abortion is merely 'a woman and her body')."[3]

That first cell begins developing in ways we're now able to detect with more certainty:

> The cardiovascular system is the first major system to function. At about 22 days after conception the child's heart begins to circulate his own blood, unique from that of his mother's, and his heartbeat can be detected on ultrasound.
>
> At just six weeks, the child's eyes and eyelids, nose, mouth, and tongue have formed.
>
> Electrical brain activity can be detected at six or seven weeks, and by the end of the eighth week, the child, now known scientifically as a 'fetus,' has developed all of his organs and bodily structures.
>
> By ten weeks after conception the child can make bodily movements."[4]

All of which led pro-life activist Ashley McGuire to observe, "when you're seeing a baby sucking its thumb at 18 weeks, smiling, clapping, it becomes harder to square the idea that that 20-week-old, that unborn baby or fetus, is discardable."[5]

That's an observation resonating with laypeople and medical professionals alike. Colleen Malloy, a neonatologist and faculty member at Northwestern University, said, "The more I advanced in my field of neonatology, the more it just became the logical choice to recognize the developing fetus for what it is: a fetus, instead of some sort of subhuman form. It just became so obvious that these were just developing humans."[6]

Malloy also recognized the irony that "medical teams spend enormous effort, time, and money to deliver babies safely and nurse premature infants back to health. Yet physicians often support abortion, even late into fetal development."[7]

That irony is a reminder that the debate over abortion should focus on abortion itself, not the circumstances surrounding it. If what's terminated is a life, then questions should be raised about that life's value, with important yet secondary questions raised about the difficulties that life may cause.

In fact, despite the claims that pro-life views dismiss the needs of women and are inherently sexist, a number of past and current feminists are strongly pro-life, and it's fascinating to read what pioneers like Susan B. Anthony and Pearl Buck had to say about abortion.[8]

ROE V. WADE

The landmark Supreme Court case of 1973 shifted the focus of the abortion debate onto issues of privacy, autonomy, and a potential mother's well-being. Those issues, and an ever-expanding way of framing them, have dominated the national discussion.

Roe v. Wade developed the trimester concept, giving women an unqualified right to abort during the first three months (first trimester) of pregnancy. Some government regulation could then be allowed during the second trimester, and states could restrict or even ban abortions in the final three months.[9]

Even then, during the last trimester, *Roe* determined an abortion could be obtained if a doctor certified it as necessary to save a mother's life or health.[10]

This 7–2 decision rested on the right to privacy, a right not found in the Constitution but articulated in an earlier SCOTUS decision. In 1965's *Griswold v. Connecticut*, Justice William O. Douglas wrote that a general right to privacy can be found in "zones" created by the First, Third, Fourth, and Ninth Amendments.[11]

Eight years later, that "right to privacy" would be cited by SCOTUS as having roots in the Fourteenth Amendment, which states in part, "nor shall any State deprive any person of life, liberty, or property, without due process of law; nor deny to any person within its jurisdiction the equal protection of the laws."[12]

In light of that, the Court ruled, "This right of privacy…founded in the Fourteenth Amendment's concept of personal liberty and restrictions upon state action…is broad enough to encompass a woman's decision whether or not to terminate her pregnancy."[13] Since then, nearly sixty million lives have been terminated. Sixty million cries never heard; sixty million tears never shed.

The wisdom of this decision is still questioned, not just by conservative scholars but liberal, pro-choice ones as well.

"One of the most curious things about *Roe*," said Laurence Tribe (a professor at Harvard University who supports *Roe*) "is that, behind its own verbal smokescreen, the substantive judgments on which it rests are nowhere to be found."[14]

The past dean of Stanford Law School, John Hart Ely, concurred, saying *Roe v. Wade* "is not constitutional law and gives almost no sense of an obligation to try to be. What is frightening about *Roe* is that this super-protected right is not inferable from the language of the Constitution."[15]

Even the late Supreme Court justice Ruth Bader Ginsburg wrote in 1985, "The Court presented an incomplete justification for its action… the Court's *Roe* position is weakened…by the opinion's concentration on a medically approved autonomy idea, to the exclusion of a constitutionally based sex-equality perspective."[16]

Nearly a half century after it was handed down, *Roe v Wade* has hardly settled the abortion controversy and has, in fact, largely contributed to it.

THE HEALTH OF THE MOTHER IN QUESTION

In response to a request for information about the number of abortions performed to protect a woman's health, the Connecticut Department of Health made an interesting observation:

> Neither state or federal law nor regulations define the phrase "preserving the life or health of the woman." *We were unable to find any governmental guidelines on the issue.* Representatives from various health and abortion agencies suggest both state and federal laws leave the definition of "preserving the life or health of the pregnant woman" up to the expectant mother's physician [emphasis mine].[17]

The life or health of a woman seeking an abortion, then, is not a question of life or death, nor of verifiable health or illness, as it would seem at face value. It is, instead, subject to interpretation and determined by consensus between the patient and her physician. It could mean something as severe as bodily threat or something as minor as inconvenience.

No wonder, then, an article appearing in the ethics guide for the BBC notes:

> The self-defence argument for abortion seems to fail here, because although a threat to life can be a defence to a charge of killing someone, none of the above [damage to mental health, family, career prospects, financial prospects, or plans for her life] would be an adequate defence in a case of homicide, nor would they be regarded as reasons that justified euthanasia.[18]

THE BACK-ALLEY SCENARIO

The thought of desperate women seeking illegal abortions at the hands of back-alley butchers is enough to sway some to a pro-choice view. It makes the case that women will get abortions whether they're legal or illegal, so we have to choose: will they have access to safe procedures, or risk disease or death because unsafe conditions were the only options?

The back-alley nightmare is an effective specter to raise. It's also a manipulation that should be examined more closely.

Prominent abortion provider Dr. Bernard Nathanson, one of the founders of the National Abortion Rights Action League (NARAL) made a stunning admission on the subject:

> How many deaths were we talking about when abortion was illegal? In NARAL, we generally emphasized the frame of the individual case, not the mass statistics, but when we spoke of the latter it was always "5,000 to 10,000 deaths a year." I confess that I knew the figures were totally false,

and I suppose the others did too if they stopped to think of it. But in the "morality" of our revolution, it was a useful figure, widely accepted, so why go out of our way to correct it with honest statistics? The overriding concern was to get the laws eliminated, and anything within reason that had to be done was permissible.[19]

Another pro-abortion spokesperson Marian Faux justified the dishonest tactic when she wrote, "An image of tens of thousands of women being maimed or killed each year by illegal abortion was so persuasive a piece of propaganda that the [pro-abortion] movement could be forgiven its failure to double-check the facts."[20]

Activist Malcolm Potts agreed, admitting, "Those who want the [abortion] law to be liberalized will stress the hazards of illegal abortion and claim that hundreds, or thousands, of women die unnecessarily each year when the actual number is far lower."[21] Even *Sisterhood Is Powerful*, described as the "neo-feminist Bible," criticizes the "10,000 Women Die of Illegal Abortions" exaggeration: "A study made in the 1930s, before the development of antibiotics made even illegal abortion less deadly than it used to be, came up with this number of 10,000 deaths; but it is no longer anywhere near the truth and has no place in any serious discussion of abortion."[22]

LATE-TERM HORRORS

But if the nightmare of women suffering from illegal abortions has been inflated, the horror of late-term abortion seems to have been understated.

Between 2003 and 2014, the Centers for Disease Control (CDC), in an attempt to determine the number of live births accidentally resulting from abortions, identified 143 cases in which a child had been born alive during an abortion and died afterwards. A recitation of the figures is chilling: "About 42 percent of the deaths occurred within an hour of birth, 54 percent occurred between one and 23 hours after birth, and about 4 percent of the deaths occurred a day after birth."[23]

Another report by Minnesota's health department in 2017 found that "three infants were born alive during the course of an abortion in 2017, but later died. *In two of those cases, no care was given.* In one of those two, the infant's vital signs were already weak" (emphasis mine).[24]

Arizona health authorities reported in 2017 that ten infants were born alive during abortions, but the journalist covering the story added ominously: "Physicians submitted statements about the level of care provided in each case, but those statements aren't detailed in Arizona's report."[25]

Florida also reported that eleven infants were born alive during attempted abortions in 2017, and six were born in 2018, with another born the following year. Yet again: "Details aren't available in the reports."[26]

BUT WHY? REASONS AND REGRETS

Although worst-case scenarios are often presented when people argue for the right to abort (a woman raped who becomes pregnant; a victim of incest impregnated by a father) the facts present much less compelling scenarios that question how accurately the term "life and health of the mother" is being applied.

According to the pro-choice advocacy organization the Guttmacher Institute, the most often cited reasons women give for an abortion include:

- Having a baby would dramatically interfere with education, work, or ability to care for their dependents.

- Inability to afford a baby at the time.

- Lack of choice because of limited resources and existing responsibilities to others.[27]

All of which can be sympathized with; none of which compel the killing of an innocent young life. Which may be the reason 6,469 women and men testified to "abortion regret" in "The Silent No More

Campaign" video, a project of Priests for Life and Anglicans for Life.[28] It may also account for the number of women who've contributed stories of their post-abortion grief to the website "Voices of Women Who Mourn."[29]

Despite the pride some women have displayed by wearing "I Had an Abortion" T-shirts,[30] other women clearly experienced something other than pride in the aftermath of their abortions.

Yet a 2020 study reported in *Social Science and Medicine* reported that among women surveyed who'd had abortions, five years after the fact the majority felt relief and a conviction they'd done the right thing.[31]

This, along with statistics from the Pew Research Forum showing one-third of Americans believe abortion should be illegal[32] and Gallup reports showing 53 percent of women and 43 percent of men identify as pro-choice,[33] proves how utterly unsettled we are over such a vital issue.

KEEP IN MIND

The following general points are significant when considering abortion from a biblical worldview:

1. We are being told that defense of the unborn is an expression of sexism, and therefore should be silenced. But many people who are pro-choice know little about when life begins, so they view abortion as a means of birth control. Discussing life at conception is critical.

2. Some will assume if you are pro-life, you must be indifferent to the plight of women in crisis pregnancy. Stressing compassion and consideration for women is important, without compromising the priority life takes.

3. If the discussion is about abortion, then the abortion procedure and the object of the procedure should be the focus of the discussion. Is it a life at conception, and if so, is life disposable?

4. *Roe v. Wade* cited a right to privacy not found in the Constitution, and continues to be a source of debate, even among scholars and justices who are pro-choice.

5. Scientific advances over the past decades have strengthened pro-life arguments considerably, making it harder to view the unborn simply as a "fetus." The image of a child in the womb verifies that it is, indeed, a child in the womb.

KEEP IT BIBLICAL

The following points are significant when examining abortion from a biblical worldview:

1. The child in the womb was foreknown and foreordained by God.

> "Before I formed you in the womb I knew you;
> Before you were born I sanctified you;
> I ordained you a prophet to the nations."
> (Jeremiah 1:5)

2. The child in the womb was fashioned in uniqueness by God.

> My frame was not hidden from You,
> When I was made in secret,
> And skillfully wrought in the lowest parts of the earth.
> Your eyes saw my substance, being yet unformed.
> And in Your book they all were written,
> The days fashioned for me,
> When as yet there were none of them.
> (Psalm 139:15-16)

3. The child in the womb is capable of feelings, even those of joy.

> And it happened, when Elizabeth heard the greeting of
> Mary, that the babe leaped in her womb; and Elizabeth

was filled with the Holy Spirit. Then she spoke out with a loud voice and said, "Blessed are you among women, and blessed is the fruit of your womb! But why is this granted to me, that the mother of my Lord should come to me? For indeed, as soon as the voice of your greeting sounded in my ears, the babe leaped in my womb for joy" (Luke 1:41-44).

4. Since the preborn are foreknown and fashioned by God, capable of feeling and ongoing development, they qualify as dependent, vulnerable lives deserving protection.

> Defend the poor and fatherless;
> Do justice to the afflicted and needy.
> Deliver the poor and needy;
> Free them from the hand of the wicked.
> (Psalm 82:3-4)

5. Since the preborn are the smallest and most vulnerable members of the human race, they qualify as those to whom Jesus said we have a responsibility.

> "And the King will answer and say to them, 'Assuredly, I say to you, inasmuch as you did it to one of the least of these My brethren, you did it to Me'" (Matthew 25:40).

KEEP IT GOING

The following are some of the questions or arguments you're likely to hear when discussing abortion, along with some suggested points for keeping the discussion going.

"A woman has the right to decide what to do with her own body."

1. All of us have that right, but with limits. There are lots of things I can't do with my own body because of the impact

they'll have on others. I can't shoot you with my own body. I can't steal from you with my own body. Bodily autonomy stops when it damages another.

2. If abortion were an act a woman committed only on her own body, then I wouldn't object. But there is another body involved.

3. Sex between consenting adults is a private matter. Protecting a life that results is a public matter.

"The Supreme Court decided in favor of abortion back in 1973, so this issue is settled."

1. Technically, the Supreme Court decided women have unlimited right to an abortion only during their first trimester of pregnancy. Restrictions could still be imposed during the second and third trimesters.

2. A number of legal scholars, including the late Supreme Court justice Ruth Bader Ginsburg, seriously questioned the legitimacy of the SCOTUS decision.

3. Given that more than one-third of Americans believe abortion should be illegal, the issue is hardly "settled."

"No one knows when life begins, so you can't say abortion is murder."

1. When the sperm fertilizes the egg at conception, the resulting zygote is made of DNA and other human particles. It is unquestionably human and alive.

2. Since the zygote is made of DNA, it includes hereditary attributes and unique design. It is unquestionably human, alive, and unique.

3. The zygote starts developing immediately and will keep

developing from conception to birth to death. It is unquestionably human, alive, unique, and a work in progress.

"If abortion is made illegal, women will go back to having back-alley abortions and dying as a result."

1. Pro-abortion activists have admitted that the reported number of women dying of back-alley abortions was always wildly inflated.

2. Would you really strike down laws against selling drugs, assault, or murder, just because people might resort to doing these crimes in a back alley? We don't decriminalize behaviors just so they'll be done more safely.

3. One woman dying of a botched abortion is one too many. But one child dying of any kind of abortion is also one too many.

4. If a life is being taken, it's being taken whether the environment is filthy or pristine.

5. Abortion is never an inevitability. If *Roe v. Wade* were reversed, that alone would not force women to seek abortions illegally. There will always be other options, and we should help women find them and choose them.

"A man has no right to speak about this. No uterus, no opinion."

1. Abortion is not a female issue or a male issue. It's a human issue.

2. If a woman is taking a human life, do you honestly think only another woman should be allowed to intervene, and a man should have nothing to say about it?

3. Men should never speak casually about what a woman in

an unwanted or a crisis pregnancy goes through, because they cannot know. But that doesn't negate their opinion on whether or not another life is involved, and whether or not that preborn life has a right to ongoing life.

"If a woman is raped and becomes pregnant, should she be forced to have the baby?"

1. If a child is conceived in rape, should it be forced to die?

2. Is the child conceived in rape of less value than the child conceived in love?

3. The choice between hardship for one person and death for another is a horrendous one. But if it has to be made, the hardship of one is preferable to the death of another.

"If a woman is impregnated because of incest, should she be forced to have the baby?"

1. If a child is conceived through incest, should it be forced to die?

2. Is the child conceived through incest of less value than the child conceived in love?

3. The choice between hardship for one person and death for another is a horrendous one. But if it has to be made, the hardship of one is preferable to the death of another.

"Should the life of the mother be sacrificed for the life of the child?"

1. No. Most of us holding pro-life views don't believe that a pregnancy should be carried to full term if the physical life of the mother is seriously and verifiably threatened. The choice, in that case, should be the mother's.

2. If by "the life of the mother" you mean the emotional well-being or the circumstances involved, then physical life is a higher priority than emotional or situational well-being. In that case the mother is making a sacrifice, and a huge one, but that's a better option than the child's life literally being sacrificed.

3. No one's negating what a woman having an unwanted pregnancy will have to go through, and we should all work together to keep unwanted pregnancies from happening. But if one happens, and one party's right to live is pitted against another party's relief from crisis, then the right to live takes the higher priority.

"Should women who have abortions be considered criminal?"

1. No, because the woman having an abortion has not broken the law. I believe abortion is immoral, but not unlawful.

2. I would like to see *Roe v. Wade* overturned, and yes, I would like abortions to be outlawed because I believe they involve the taking of an innocent life.

3. I am not qualified to say what the consequence for having an abortion should be, and since we are far from *Roe v. Wade* being overturned, that's not an issue we need to solve at this time anyway.

4. We can believe something is wrong and should be outlawed without knowing what the legal consequence for it should be.

"Can't you respect the fact that a woman who had an abortion probably struggled with her decision and did not make it easily?"

1. Absolutely, I do respect that. I assume she thought the decision through and probably struggled with it. It can't have

been an easy one to make. But that doesn't mean it was the right decision.

2. Studies show that the majority of women having abortions aren't doing so for life-threatening reasons, but more for reasons having to do with work, career, or economics. Those issues are serious, for sure, but not more serious than a child's right to live.

"It's inconsistent for people to say they're pro-life, and then turn around and support policies that are inhumane."

1. You're right. Pro-life should be an all-encompassing ethic, not one applied to birth only.

2. We may disagree, though, on what constitutes "policies that are inhumane." Can you help me understand which policies you're referring to so I can get a better idea of where we agree or disagree?

"Plenty of women who've had abortions say they are glad they did and that their lives took a much better course as a result."

1. Do we ever decide if something's right or wrong based on how people feel after they've done it? If I stole some money and was glad I did, and if my life took a better course as a result, would that make it right?

2. Some studies indicate that women who've had abortions can be subject to serious depression and even consider suicide.

3. There's a considerable number of women who say they're glad they had an abortion. There's also a considerable number of women who say they deeply regret having an abortion.

"Condemning abortion is just another way of men trying to control women!"

1. It's a mistake to make this simply a male versus female issue. A number of early feminists were against abortion, and a number of modern feminists are too.

2. In the latest Gallup poll, 43 percent of men surveyed described themselves as pro-choice. It seems nearly half the men surveyed had no desire to control women through abortion.

3. Men who want to control women may do so by preventing them from having an abortion or by coercing them to have an abortion. Most women and men who condemn abortion want no control over women. They want protection for the unborn.

"Plenty of women who've had abortions go on to give birth later in life, so they obviously do love children and aren't murderers."

1. No one's suggesting that women who have abortions hate children. Women who have abortions may be terminating a life without even realizing it's a life.

2. The wrongness in abortion is in determining which preborn child has a right to live and which does not.

3. You can love one life and still be responsible for ending another.

"If your religion condemns abortion, then don't have an abortion. But don't tell others not to just because your church says it's a sin."

1. Some religious beliefs should not be imposed. But some, like the belief that we should not kill, should be imposed

because it's not just a religious issue. It's a human rights issue apart from religion.

2. I doubt you'd ever say, "If your religion condemns racism, then don't be a racist. But don't tell others not to just because your church says racism is a sin."

3. Christianity condemns indifference to the poor, sexism, violence, and abortion. We're against all of these and want to do what we can to prevent all of them.

4. I believe God places high value on every life, a value we should honor from the moment a life is conceived. Talking with you, I'm glad God made you, and I'm glad your mother carried you all the way.

> *"And if we can accept that a mother can kill even her own child, how can we tell other people not to kill one another? How do we persuade a woman not to have an abortion? As always, we must persuade her with love…And we remind ourselves that love means to be willing to give until it hurts."*
>
> MOTHER TERESA

CHAPTER SEVEN

THE CROSS AND THE RAINBOW

Discussing Homosexuality

On June 26, 2015, the Supreme Court of the United States ruled 5–4 that state laws prohibiting same-sex marriage were unconstitutional. The decision signaled a sea change in our national understanding of family, sending the message that homosexual unions have been officially normalized.

Another pointed message went out when President Obama had the White House bathed in rainbow-colored lights for days afterwards, telling the American people, "The issue is not only decided, but officially celebrated by your commander-in-chief and his family." If you weren't celebrating, you were out of step.

But you were also reassured, in the words of the SCOTUS majority opinion, that your right to express and practice your beliefs would still be protected:

> Finally, it must be emphasized that religions, and those who adhere to religious doctrines, may continue to advocate with utmost, sincere conviction that, by divine

precepts, same-sex marriage should not be condoned. The
First Amendment ensures that religious organizations and
persons are given proper protection as they seek to teach
the principles that are so fulfilling and so central to their
lives and faiths, and to their own deep aspirations to continue the family structure they have long revered.[1]

That sounded fair. The rights of religious organizations and individuals to "seek and teach" our principles about sex and family were
still protected. We could even advocate, with "sincere conviction," that
same-sex marriage should not be condoned. No worries.

Then the California State Assembly entertained a bill that would
make it illegal for a Christian counselor to charge for services if he
helped a repentant homosexual abstain.[2] Then a presidential aspirant
said all churches that do not affirm homosexuality should lose their
tax-exempt status.[3] Then a president-elect met with a group advising
him to strip Christian schools and universities of their accreditation if
they don't change their policies on LGBTQ.[4] Then the California State
Assembly passed a resolution advising pastors and Christian counselors to avoid telling homosexuals they can change.[5]

It's become difficult to square current trends with past Supreme
Court reassurances about First Amendment rights, and that is the sub-
stance of what we face when we address homosexuality today. On this
issue, above all others mentioned in this book, we're compelled not
only to explain our beliefs, nor just to defend our beliefs, but also to
defend our right to hold and practice those beliefs, as a growing segment of society comes to view them as harmful.

This colors our relations with family members, close friends, and
associates who hold pro-gay views, because the intolerance of the university has trickled into the mainstream, poisoning relations between
"woke" young people and their parents, gay and lesbian people and their
families, and social justice warriors and anyone they condemn.

Modern condemnation of the biblical view on sexuality often
comes in the form of (1) belief in the inborn nature of homosexuality, (2) the number of churches becoming "gay affirming," and (3) the

number of churches making this a secondary issue. These issues are the ones you're likely to confront when discussing homosexuality.

INBORN AND INTENDED

Since 1991, the public has routinely been informed that yet another study indicates homosexuality is inborn. Initially these reports were hailed by activists as validation, because if gays were born that way, then God or nature must have intended it so.

But over the past three decades, the methodology, conclusions, and interpretations of these studies have repeatedly been challenged and defended, as groups have squared off over their validity. The gay-affirming camp has claimed victory because the studies allegedly proved homosexuality was not a choice and, if God exists, it must therefore be something He created. Non-affirmers have retorted that the jury is still out (true), the studies are not conclusive (also true), and that homosexuality couldn't be inborn because God wouldn't create a sinful tendency (half true, since sinful tendencies could be inborn, but God did not create them).

With time, as LGBTQ advances have accelerated, there's been less debate because there's less need. Studies indicate the majority of Americans don't find homosexuality immoral.[6] Since the public is largely convinced, the argument intended to convince became less crucial. After all, people are not likely to care what causes something they're already OK with.

Now the push to *prove* homosexuality is inborn has been replaced with the *assumption* it's inborn. Repeated for decades in the spin cycle, the public presumes so many talking heads can't be wrong so it must be true, not because it's been proven but because it's been repeated.

This accounts for the angry response Christian friends and family members get when they share their views. "How can you say something I was born with, something God obviously made me to be, is wrong?" they hear from offended loved ones. Which raises two questions: Has it been proven that homosexuality is inborn? If it has been proven, does that prove homosexuality is God-ordained?

The conventional "born gay" wisdom seems born more of repetition than examination. Despite the many studies offering evidence (not proof), the American Psychological Association has established that "sexual orientation has not been conclusively found to be determined by any particular factor or factors."[7] Elaborating on this, the APA continues:

> There is no consensus among scientists about the exact reasons that an individual develops a heterosexual, bisexual, gay or lesbian orientation. Although much research has examined the possible genetic, hormonal, developmental, social and cultural influences on sexual orientation, no findings have emerged that permit scientists to conclude that sexual orientation is determined by any particular factor or factors.[8]

When the APA cannot say conclusively what causes homosexuality, it's also saying that no one theory, including the "inborn theory," is undisputed. As University of Michigan professor of psychology and women's studies Sari van Anders observes, "The science of whether sexual orientation is biological is pretty sparse and full of disparate, mixed and unreplicated findings."[9]

Pro-gay activists were wrong in asserting that homosexuality is proven to be inborn. They were also wrong when they argued that if something is inborn, it must be healthy, since there may also be inborn predispositions to alcoholism, chemical dependency, depression, and even violence. Nothing is legitimized just because it's inborn.

But conservatives were also wrong in assuming they needed to prove homosexuality is *not* inborn because the cause of homosexuality doesn't determine its normality or abnormality. Worldview, not genes, settles that question. According to a biblical worldview, we are all created by God, but we're not all God created us to be.

CHURCHES CONVERTING OR CONVERGING

Well-known evangelical converts to a gay-affirming view of the Bible include sociologist Tony Campolo, popular author Jen Hatmaker, the late Rachel Held Evans, former Mars Hill pastor and author

Rob Bell, and ethicist David Gushee. All have embraced a pro-gay interpretation of the Bible that revises the meaning of verses assumed to condemn homosexuality.[10]

Whole denominations have been making a similar shift, including the Presbyterian Church USA, the Evangelical Lutheran Church of America, and the Episcopalian Church, along with individual congregations formerly associated with the Southern Baptist Convention, the Assemblies of God, and the Vineyard Fellowship.

All of which leads gay friends and loved ones to ask, "If so many Bible-believing Christians are seeing the light, why can't you?"

The convergence of other evangelical leaders and groups can incite similar questions. Not quite converting to a pro-gay position, they bring the pro-gay and anti-gay positions together in a "let's get along" convergence by saying, "Hey, you're a Christian believing gay is OK, I'm a Christian who disagrees, but who cares? We're all one in Christ."

The widely respected author Max Lucado took this approach with Jen Hatmaker, appearing on her podcast to discuss how Christians can get along when they disagree. Knowing she promoted a pro-gay interpretation of the Bible and that there was wide-spread controversy over her conversion to that position, he noted:

"And so you and I, when it comes to the table, whether literally the Lord's table, or figuratively the community table, you're my sister, and I'm your brother…But if you and I both call God our god, and Jesus our savior-brother, the Holy Spirit our power, the Father our strength. If we agree on those big rocks, then we got to figure out a way to be together. And so I think that's step number one, it's not an option."[11]

One of modern Christianity's most prominent voices thereby declared that Christians who condone homosexuality (in theory or practice) and Christians who don't must "find a way to be together." Unity above all; but truth about sexual ethics? Optional.

This, too, complicates matters when gay loved ones, hearing remarks like Lucado's, appeal to us, "Why not relax about all this?"

We can agree to disagree with nonbelievers, certainly. But among believers, we can't. There are, of course, issues we needn't divide over. Christians who believe in a pretribulation rapture needn't break fellowship with Christians who don't. Those holding the eternal security view can worship comfortably with their Arminian brethren. But there are some issues so vital that within the church, they demand agreement or withdrawal. Homosexuality is one of them.

Sexual sin is a primary issue, named and condemned in twenty-two of the twenty-seven books of the New Testament. It is cited as the sole justification for divorce (Matthew 5:31-32), the reason for the first recorded excommunication (1 Corinthians 5), and a cause for literal withdrawal of interpersonal fellowship (1 Corinthians 5:11; Ephesians 5:11-12).

Plainly put, there is no biblical precedent or justification for gay-affirming believers and traditional believers to attempt unity. We can, as Paul said, interact respectfully with nonbelievers who engage in any number of sexual sins (1 Corinthians 5:9-10). But when it comes to believers, rejection of basic doctrines on sex and morality make it impossible for us to "find a way to be together." Apologist Alisa Childers, reacting to Lucado's endorsement of Hatmaker, underscores this point:

> Can you imagine a shepherd trying to 'build a bridge' or 'sit at the same table' with a wolf? When a wolf comes after the sheep, the shepherd has one job. Protect the sheep. Not the wolf…The gospel is worth fighting for. The church is worth protecting. It's this generation's turn to do the hard things, and I pray God will give our Christian leaders the courage and unflinching loyalty to the sufficiency and authority of the Scriptures not only to discern the deceptions, but also to speak God's truth clearly to those who are being misled.[12]

Childers's prayer hearkens back to one expressed by Charles Spurgeon so long ago and so relevant to our discussion today: "We have come to a turning point in the road. If we turn to the right mayhap our children and our children's children will go that way; but if we turn to the left, generations yet unborn will curse our names for having been unfaithful to God and to His Word."[13]

KEEP IN MIND

The following general points are significant when considering homosexuality from a biblical worldview.

1. If the person you're talking with is gay-affirming, there's a good chance he assumes you look down on lesbians and gays or that you're ignorant and have absorbed inherited prejudices. Listening respectfully, asking pertinent questions, and making your points clearly can go a long way toward diffusing those assumptions.

2. Remember, the culture has shifted, so your view is not the dominant one. If you are not gay-affirming, you are on the defense to explain why. Keep your explanation grounded in the concept that we have a Creator who loves us and created us with intentions that homosexuality, like many sexual behaviors, falls short of.

3. Avoid generalizations about lesbians and gays. None of them hold true in all cases, and generalizations will make you look uninformed and bigoted.

4. Don't assume that if someone thinks you're hateful that means you must have done something wrong. The biblical position on sexuality is often viewed as hateful, and if you've spoken truth in love and it's been misinterpreted, you're not responsible.

5. Keep your priorities straight. First, try to sustain communication. Second, if the person is a non-Christian, make the gospel the main point. Third, if the person is a professing believer, make obedience to the Word the main point.

KEEP IT BIBLICAL

The following general points are significant when examining homosexuality from a biblical worldview.

1. God's intentions for the human sexual union are made clear in both Testaments.

   > And the LORD God said, "It is not good that man should be alone; I will make him a helper comparable to him."…Therefore a man shall leave his father and mother and be joined to his wife, and they shall become one flesh (Genesis 2:18,24).

2. Human experience often falls short of God's intentions.

   > For I know that in me (that is, in my flesh) nothing good dwells; for to will is present with me, but how to perform what is good I do not find (Romans 7:18).

   > For all have sinned and fall short of the glory of God (Romans 3:23).

3. There's no intellectually honest way to get around the prohibitions of homosexuality in both Testaments (see Leviticus 18:22; 20:13; Romans 1:26-27; 1 Corinthians 6:9-10; 1 Timothy 1:8-11).

4. Former lesbians and gays were a part of the early church and did indeed change.

   > And such were some of you. But you were washed, but you were sanctified, but you were justified in the name of the Lord Jesus and by the Spirit of our God (1 Corinthians 6:11).

5. The invitation to salvation goes to everyone, but it is followed by the command to self-denying discipleship.

"For God so loved the world that He gave His only begotten Son, that whoever believes in Him should not perish but have everlasting life" (John 3:16).

"If anyone desires to come after Me, let him deny himself, and take up his cross daily, and follow Me" (Luke 9:23).

KEEP IT GOING

The following are some of the questions or arguments you're likely to hear when discussing homosexuality, along with some suggested points for keeping the discussion going.

"I was born gay, so God made me that way, and God doesn't make mistakes."

1. I can see why you'd feel that way. Most gays I know felt different from pretty early in life. Do you think that means you were born gay or could it mean you felt that way for as long as you can remember?

2. There's no proof people are born gay. Lots of studies, but no proof. Still, I'm open to whatever evidence comes up.

3. Seriously, does it matter? If you think homosexuality is right, it shouldn't matter whether or not you were born gay. Something doesn't have to be inborn to be OK. That works both ways. If I think something isn't what God intended, it doesn't matter to me whether it was inborn or acquired.

4. I think all of us have feelings we weren't meant to have. That's what the Bible talks about when it calls us a fallen race.

5. Do we decide something's right or wrong just by whatever may have caused it?

"I've tried to change but I couldn't, so I had to quit pretending and just be who I am."

1. I'm glad you don't want to pretend. No one should have to do that.

2. Can you tell me more about what happened when you tried to change? It sounds like a hard time you went through.

3. Nobody has the right to tell you to change. We don't choose our sexual orientation, we only choose what to do with it. So if you're at peace with your life, I respect that. Now, if you ask me point blank what I believe about sexuality, I won't lie to you. But I won't impose on you, either. Fair enough?

4. The big change we all need has to do with life and death, not gay or straight. Everyone's born a sinner, that's why we need to be born again. I'd love to tell you how that's played out in my own life.

5. If you're a Christian, you don't figure something's right or wrong by whether or not you can change your desire for it. If we struggle with feelings we don't want, we decide to give in to them or resist them based on what God's Word says, right? Otherwise, we'd all just go with whatever we feel.

"Every mental health association agrees there's nothing wrong with homosexuality."

1. Homosexuality's a moral issue, not a psychological one. When it comes to mental health, I don't think lesbians and gays are saner or crazier than anyone else.

2. To me the question is whether or not we have a Creator, and whether or not what we're feeling or doing is what He had in mind.

3. As a Christian, I think God inspired the writers of the Bible to help us know what He had in mind, and that's how I judge whether something's right or wrong, healthy or unhealthy.

"Every mental health association agrees gays and lesbians can't change."

1. They don't quite say that. In fact, they generally agree that sexuality can be fluid, changing over time. They do say that conscious attempts to change feelings from gay to straight have not proven to be effective in most cases.

2. It depends on how you define "change." They don't say gays and lesbians can't change their behavior, or the kinds of relationships they have, or that they can't experience any shift at all in their sexual feelings.

3. Mental health experts do say gays and lesbians should not be coerced into trying to change, and I fully agree.

"Same-sex marriage is as good as straight marriage."

1. If you mean gay and lesbian couples can love each other just as straight couples can, I agree.

2. If you mean gay and lesbian couples should have the right to form relationships as consenting adults, I agree.

3. Maybe we can get further if you tell me your concept of marriage. How do you define it?

4. I think marriage is, by design, a male-female union, both because of the way we're built and the potential for procreation. I also think there are emotional differences in our makeup as women and men, so I see marriage as a union of contrast. That makes it a oneness rather than a sameness.

5. I see a difference between a marriage and a partnership. I see marriage as a male-female covenant, and partnership as being a broader term for different kinds of committed relationships.

"Gay and lesbian couples can raise kids as well as straight couples can."

1. That depends. Sure, a relatively healthy gay couple will be better for kids than a very unhealthy straight couple.

2. If both couples are relatively healthy, then I think a man and a woman bring a natural set of parenting skills to the table that are in the best interest of the kids.

3. I don't think children are automatically damaged if they're raised by a same-sex couple. Both parties in that couple might be intelligent, hard-working, terrific people. But they're two people of the same sex, so I don't think they can provide the same range of benefits two people of the opposite sex can provide.

"If you won't attend my wedding, you're completely disrespecting my partner and me."

1. That's not fair. Don't you know how hard it is for me to say no to this? But I would never ask you to do something you don't believe in. Please don't ask that of me.

2. When you go to a wedding, it's not just because you love the people getting married. It's also because you completely believe in and support the union. Would you really want someone at your wedding who couldn't say they completely agree with it?

3. I love you too much to be fake with you. I hope you feel the

same. So don't ask me to pretend, which is what I'd be doing if I came. Let's keep our relationship strong and real, OK?

"By holding on to the view that homosexuality is a sin, you're doing serious damage to me."

1. If I have ever expressed my view in a way that's damaged you, I want to know. Please tell me, and I promise to listen and take what you say seriously.

2. I don't think it's fair to say my view itself is damaging. In any relationship, there are things about one person that the other person disagrees with or even disapproves of. That's not damaging, that's life.

3. If I impose my view on you, I'd say that's wrong. If I express my view and you express yours, that's conversation. Would you prefer we not talk about it at all? We don't have to if it's alienating us from each other.

4. If you ask me not to impose my view, I'll agree. If you ask me not to have my view, I'll respectfully refuse. If I tried telling you not to have your own view, I would hope you'd refuse too.

"Viewpoints like yours cause gay teens to hate themselves and sometimes even to kill themselves."

1. The Christian view of sex doesn't harm anyone. The way it's expressed or practiced can cause harm. It's not fair to confuse the two.

2. If someone tells a gay kid, "I love you and so does God. But I don't think that's God's best for you," that doesn't hurt him. If someone tells a gay kid, "God hates you!" that hurts. There's a big difference.

3. There are people who hurt gay teens not because they hold the Christian view but because they're hurtful people. They call gay kids names and even assault them. There's nothing biblical about that, and I'll stand with you against them any day.

"Christians were wrong about slavery and about women. They're making the same mistake today about gays and lesbians."

1. Some Christians were wrong about slavery and some fought slavery. Some Christians have been sexist but plenty have honored women. Your generalizations are not accurate.

2. If some people in a group were once wrong about something, does that mean all people in that group are now wrong about something else? That doesn't make sense.

3. Some Christians have been wrong about things in the past. You could say that about any group. Let's talk about the issue in the here and now.

"Jesus never said anything about homosexuality."

1. We can't really know either way because we don't have a complete record of everything He said. The four Gospels record a lot of His words, but they don't claim to have recorded all of them.

2. There are a lot of things Jesus didn't specifically mention, things that we still know to be wrong. His not mentioning something isn't enough to justify it.

3. He was pretty specific about God's intention for marriage being a male to female union, so even if He didn't say anything about homosexuality, He spoke clearly about the definition of marriage.

"The authors of the Bible didn't know what we know today about sexuality."

1. Are you sure? Paul and Moses, the two biblical authors who wrote about the subject, were both learned men. There's literature from Paul's time about homosexual love that he was probably familiar with, and Moses was raised in Egyptian courts. I think they both knew more about sex than you give them credit for.

2. If Moses and Paul weren't inspired directly by God, then I'd give this argument more weight. But if God directed their writings, as I believe He did, then God Himself surely knew everything we know today about sexuality, and then some!

3. For the sake of argument, let's say they didn't know what we know today about sex. If that's the case, they wrote about a number of sexual behaviors we all agree are wrong—such as adultery, incest, even bestiality—without having a modern understanding of what caused those behaviors. That alone doesn't discount their writing.

"God is love, so when people love each other, you should be glad."

1. God is also perfect and unlimited, loving everyone. He cannot love the wrong person.

2. We're imperfect and very limited, so we can definitely love the wrong person in the wrong way. I can romantically love someone other than my wife. You can romantically love someone you're supposed to be helping as a doctor or a therapist. The fact we love someone does not, in and of itself, legitimize a relationship.

3. I know you feel your relationship is loving and harms no one, so that makes it right. Many people would agree with you.

But as a Christian, I have to view a relationship not only by whether or not love is involved, but also by whether or not it's in line with what God intended. That's probably why we have different ideas about love.

"If you can't change your views, then I'll have to stay away from you, because I won't tolerate bigotry."

1. I was hoping this wouldn't come between us. It doesn't have to. People disagree and still relate. Can't we?

2. Help me understand how you define bigotry. If I think something's wrong, am I a bigot? Wouldn't I also have to think I'm better than you if I'm a bigot? Believe me, I don't.

3. If you think I'm wrong about sexuality, that's fair. But unless I treat you with disrespect or hostility, I believe the "bigot" label is way off base.

4. Bigots don't just disagree, they denigrate. They won't sit with people they're bigoted toward, they consider themselves superior to them, and they certainly don't want a relationship with them! I do want a relationship with you, I want to interact with you, and I've never said I'm better than you. Are you sure I qualify as a bigot?

5. If you withdraw from me because of this, I won't withdraw from you. As far as I'm concerned, our relationship is more important than our differences. I will always feel that way, and I hope that someday you will too.

> *"God nowhere tells us to give up things for the sake of giving them up. He tells us to give them up for the sake of the only thing worth having—viz., life with Himself."*
>
> OSWALD CHAMBERS

CHAPTER EIGHT

ETERNAL
LIVES MATTER

Discussing Race

We agree that racism is evil, but we disagree on what racism is, who gets to define it, and how that definition should be enforced. Those three points of disagreement are tearing us to shreds.

Merriam-Webster Dictionary's current attempt to define the word shows how uncertain we've become of its meaning. The first definition it offers is the one most of us know: "A belief that race is a fundamental determinant of human traits and capacities and that racial differences produce an inherent superiority of a particular race."[1]

Then it follows with an obviously recent addition: "The systemic oppression of a racial group to the social, economic, and political advantage of another," and "a political or social system founded on racism and designed to execute its principles."[2]

In an unusual move, *Merriam-Webster* then adds an explanation you won't find attached to its other definitions:

> Dictionaries are often treated as the final arbiter in arguments over a word's meaning, but they are not always well

suited for settling disputes. The lexicographer's role is to explain how words are (or have been) actually used, not how some may feel that they should be used, and they say nothing about the intrinsic nature of the thing named by a word, much less the significance it may have for individuals. When discussing concepts like racism, therefore, it is prudent to recognize that quoting from a dictionary is unlikely to either mollify or persuade the person with whom one is arguing.[3]

The source we usually turn to for a word's meaning says that when it comes to this word, the meaning is fluid. It can morph and revise according to the way people feel it should be used or the significance it may have for them. So if you want official backing for your definition, don't look here.

Where, then, should we look? When the traditional source for definitions abdicates, then the most aggressive and influential voices will fill the void. This is the point in Lewis Carroll's *Through the Looking-Glass* when Alice asks Humpty Dumpty, "Must a name mean something?" only to get the answer, "When *I* use a word…it means just what I choose it to mean—neither more nor less."[4]

CRITICAL RACE THEORY

This is where the critical race theory comes in, which is widely becoming accepted as the source for defining racism and identifying who is or is not guilty of this sin.

Advocates of the critical race theory have decided that the word *racism* means what they choose it to mean—neither more nor less. According to CRT, racism is the sin shared by all white people, by virtue of their whiteness alone, which gives them privilege and power. People of color cannot be racist because they're the minority, lacking the privilege required to be a racist. Therefore, contrary to Dr. Martin Luther King's dream of a nation where people "will not be judged by the color of their skin, but by the content of their character,"[5] CRT judges people by the color of their skin, finding them guilty without trial.

Critical race theory, like queer theory and feminist theory, has its roots in the older and broader critical theory. Developed by the Frankfurt School, a group of Marxist-influenced German intellectuals formed in the thirties,[6] critical theory aims to "overcome the social structures through which people are dominated and oppressed,"[7] while cautioning that science and other forms of objective knowledge can be tools of oppression.[8] It defines a theory as "critical" if it "seeks human emancipation from slavery" and "a world which satisfies the needs and powers" of its people.[9]

These elements of critical theory—the assumption that people are oppressed by their social structures, that objective knowledge is insufficient to achieve their liberation, and that theories seeking their emancipation are critical—show up regularly in modern identity politics and glaringly in modern discussions about race and racism.

They've actually been around for decades, especially in university settings, but have found the limelight and broad influence in recent years. I was first introduced to critical theory when I was on staff with a liberal, gay-affirming denomination in the late seventies. Feminist ministers and seminary instructors associated with the church wrote articles and preached sermons finding all men guilty of sexism and all whites guilty of racism. Their definition of discrimination was "power plus privilege," so if you were part of the majority or of the privileged group, then you were guilty.

Those of us who questioned our verdict were told that we, by virtue of our maleness or whiteness, were blinded by years of privileged conditioning. We just couldn't see our own complicity in the oppression of minorities. When we argued that we were gay, which at that time guaranteed some firsthand knowledge of minority status, we were reminded that we may have some understanding of oppression by virtue of our homosexuality, but our racial or gender privileges still made us essential players in the prejudice game. We were white, we were male, so we'd never understand. We'd always be sexist and racist, and while there was no cure, there was at least approval to be had if we'd only acknowledge, then repent of, the sin that would always plague us.

These points have been mainstreamed under the term critical race theory, developed in the seventies from the writings of Professor Derrick Bell of the University of Washington Law School.[10] According to CRT, racism is "a fundamental part of American society," where "minorities' interests are subservient to the system's self-interest," and this system, "built by and for white elites, will tolerate and encourage racial progress for minorities only if this promotes the majority's self-interest."[11] Because racism is interwoven throughout American society, and because whites are the primary beneficiaries of this systemic injustice, whites are considered racist by virtue of the privilege they have.

George Floyd's death in early 2020 fueled a massive rage at society in general, and whites in particular. This offered critical race theory an opportunity to expand its visibility by offering itself as the identifier of, and solution to, the problem of racism. It also gave CRT a juggernaut platform for exposure beyond academia, through the Black Lives Matter movement.

Black Lives Matter was founded in 2013 by Patrisse Cullors, Alicia Garza, and Opal Tometi,[12] all of them "trained Marxists," according to Ms. Cullors.[13] It's stated goal is "to eradicate white supremacy and build local power to intervene in violence inflicted on Black communities by the state and vigilantes,"[14] and its breathtaking success at mainstreaming itself was verified in 2020 when BLM's founders were named by *Time* magazine as three of "The 100 Most Influential People in the World."[15]

Despite its terrorist tactics,[16] its admission that it "disrupt(s) the Western-prescribed nuclear family structure requirement,"[17] and its self-identified Marxist roots, BLM remains a movement American culture has largely and enthusiastically embraced.

The name itself is irresistible, so people who might reject the philosophy and tactics of Black Lives Matter will still say black lives matter, as they should. That, along with the movement's undeniable intimidation factor, brings unwilling or unaware converts into the fold, marching alongside the true believers.

Dissent is prohibited, an intolerance drawn from the playbook of CRT's father, Derrick Bell, who along with numerous colleagues opposed free speech as a tool of oppression, and viewed the First Amendment as something needing reinterpretation.[18]

So discussing race today means defending traditional ideas of equality against a new framework that claims racism is not an individual problem but a collective one requiring collective remedies. An entire race is guilty. An entire system needs overhauling by any means necessary, including broad-based re-education, defunding of police or other targeted institutions, reparations to all African Americans impacted by slavery or discrimination, and wealth redistribution. Rules of engagement such as open debate and civil discourse are discarded because the goal is holy, and when it comes to fighting racism, the end justifies the means.

AND YET ...

The fact that a problem is misrepresented does not make the problem nonexistent. Nor does the fact that people are pointing out the problem in all the wrong ways mean the problem itself should be ignored. If an innocent person is getting beat up, and I scream, "This person is being murdered and all of you are guilty!," then the fact that I exaggerated the assault and wrongly accused an entire group does not mean the assault is not happening. Nor does it mean an innocent person is not being victimized, nor does it mean that there is no guilty party. Sins responded to in the wrong way are still, after all, sins.

Because of the outrageous tactics or unfair accusations often made by groups opposing racism, it can be tempting to tune them out and, in the process, dismiss the problem as nonexistent or irrelevant. That's a serious mistake, not to mention a sin in its own right.

Racism exists. The denigration of minorities, expressed in hateful words, unjust treatment, and violent actions, is not a thing of the past. To deny this is to turn a blind eye to the real and prevalent suffering of people we claim to love and respect.

White supremist groups exist openly and thrive.[19] Less open are the attitudes many privately harbor towards minorities, occasionally caught on camera, making the problem of modern prejudice undeniable.[20]

But if you as a member of a minority realize there's a percentage of the population that genuinely sees you as inferior, that realization is all the more horrible when you consider that some within that percentage have the power to pull you over, detain you, and use force against you at their discretion.

One of the worst aspects of modern discussions on racism is the demonization of police officers. Considering the sacrifice and danger inherent in their work, and the way the vast majority of them conduct themselves in circumstances unimaginable to most of us, I remain convinced that some the best women and men in our nation serve on our police forces.

But as is true of any group, some (though few) are infected with racism.[21]

So before downplaying the reality that many minorities (African-Americans in particular) face regularly, imagine knowing, each time you get behind the wheel, that you could be pulled over. Imagine also knowing that although the vast majority of officers are honorable women and men, you could have the misfortune of being pulled over by one who views you as inferior. Now imagine you are largely at the mercy of this individual, not knowing whether he or she is one of the many who is essentially decent and good, or one of the few who can and perhaps will abuse his or her authority over you.

Imagine you have lived most of your life with that reality.

Hold that thought, and the feeling it produces, when discussing racism with someone who routinely lives out what you can only imagine.

Because we know that what we see is always the tip of the iceberg, we can only imagine how many women and men cling to racist views, passing them on to their children and infecting others in their circle of influence.

To which the church should respond loudly and clearly: "Black lives, created in the image of God and of eternal value, do indeed matter. They matter to God; they matter to us; they should matter to all."

KEEP IN MIND

The following general points are significant when considering race controversies from a biblical worldview.

1. Modern excesses, done in the name of combatting racism, are ultimately the fruit of epic crimes committed against people of color. Had there not been the full-scale enslavement, then ongoing degradation of African-Americans, we'd have been spared the modern excesses of Black Lives Matter and the critical race theory. We did not commit those crimes, but they were committed, and the consequences are vast and long-term.

2. Critical race theory emphasizes "lived experience" above objective arguments, and the lived experiences of the oppressed minority are said to carry more weight than those of the oppressors. By this standard, the life stories of people of color cannot be scrutinized or challenged and must be accepted as factual.

3. CRT insists that all whites are racist and need to recognize and disown their racism. They then need to be re-educated and evangelize other whites to be similarly converted, all with the knowledge that they will never overcome their sin and must make it their life work to continuously deal with it.

4. The church is being asked to embrace CRT as true and to make its demands a priority of modern Christian living. Prominent Christian denominations and leaders are already complying, introducing Bible-believing congregations to CRT's premises.

5. CRT calls for the eradication of racism to become a top priority, yet also claims racism cannot be overcome and therefore can never be eradicated. This guarantees that the self-perpetuating industry of anti-racist education and efforts will always thrive.

KEEP IT BIBLICAL

The following points are significant when examining race controversies from a biblical worldview.

1. The entire witness of Scripture calls for just treatment of all people, while condemning racism in all forms.

   > "You shall do no injustice in judgment. You shall not be partial to the poor, nor honor the person of the mighty. In righteousness you shall judge your neighbor" (Leviticus 19:15).

   > The righteous considers the cause of the poor,
   > But the wicked does not understand such knowledge.
   > (Proverbs 29:7)

   > Learn to do good;
   > Seek justice,
   > Rebuke the oppressor;
   > Defend the fatherless,
   > Plead for the widow.
   > (Isaiah 1:17)

2. In contrast to CRT, the Bible declares all people have a sin nature, but no people have the right to predetermine what anyone else's specific sins are. For someone to be guilty of a specific sin, they must have expressed or committed that sin.

   > For all have sinned and fall short of the glory of God (Romans 3:23).

   > "Judge not, that you be not judged" (Matthew 7:1).

   > Who are you to judge another's servant? To his own master he stands or falls. Indeed, he will be made to stand, for God is able to make him stand (Romans 14:4).

3. In contrast to CRT, the Bible condemns using natural means to coerce people into a cause or belief, even if the cause is just or the belief is good.

> "My kingdom is not of this world" (John 18:36).

> For the weapons of our warfare are not carnal but mighty in God for pulling down strongholds (2 Corinthians 10:4).

> And a servant of the Lord must not quarrel but be gentle to all, able to teach, patient, in humility correcting those who are in opposition, if God perhaps will grant them repentance, so that they may know the truth (2 Timothy 2:24-25).

4. In contrast to CRT, the Bible views racism as the sin of an individual, the fruit of the sin nature rather than systemic, and a sin that can be overcome through faith in Christ and the sanctification of the Holy Spirit.

> "For out of the heart proceed evil thoughts, murders, adulteries, fornications, thefts, false witness, blasphemies" (Matthew 15:19).

> And even as they did not like to retain God in their knowledge, God gave them over to a debased mind, to do those things which are not fitting; being filled with all unrighteousness, sexual immorality, wickedness, covetousness, maliciousness; full of envy, murder, strife, deceit, evil-mindedness; they are whisperers, backbiters, haters of God, violent, proud, boasters, inventors of evil things, disobedient to parents, undiscerning, untrustworthy, unloving, unforgiving, unmerciful (Romans 1:28-31).

> And such were some of you. But you were washed, but you were sanctified, but you were justified in the name

of the Lord Jesus and by the Spirit of our God (1 Corinthians 6:11).

For sin shall not have dominion over you (Romans
6:14).

5. We are called to hear and weep with the oppressed but not to
automatically legitimize a complaint just because it comes
from a member of a historically oppressed group.

"Thus says the LORD of hosts:
'Execute true justice,
Show mercy and compassion
Everyone to his brother.
Do not oppress the widow or the fatherless,
The alien or the poor.
Let none of you plan evil in his heart
Against his brother.'"
(Zechariah 7:9-10)

Rejoice with those who rejoice, and weep with those
who weep (Romans 12:15).

He who answers a matter before he hears it,
It is folly and shame to him.
(Proverbs 18:13)

Diverse weights and diverse measures,
They are both alike, an abomination to the LORD.
(Proverbs 20:10)

KEEP IT GOING

The following are some of the questions or arguments you're likely
to hear when discussing race, along with some suggested points for
keeping the discussion going.

"Have you repented of your racism?"

1. Can you help me understand why you believe I am racist, and how you define racism? Maybe that can help us better understand each other.

2. I see racism as the belief that one race is superior to another, and the words and actions that stem from that belief. Racism is evil, for sure, and God only knows how much destruction it's caused.

3. Since I don't believe one race is superior to another, and I'm not aware of saying or doing anything to express that belief, then I really don't believe I'm guilty of racism.

4. I can only repent of sins I know I am guilty of.

5. Please tell me what I have said or done that shows I believe one race is better or worse than another.

"As a white person, you aren't able to see your own racism."

1. I'm sure there are sinful thoughts or feelings I have that I'm not aware of. That's why David said, "Who can understand his errors? Cleanse me from secret faults" (Psalm 19:12).

2. I think we can assume all people have sin in their hearts. But what we can't do is presume which sins they have, which is one reason Jesus said not to judge (Matthew 7:1-3).

3. I assume you have some thoughts or feelings that are wrong, but I don't have the ability to read your mind and tell you what they are. That works both ways.

4. I'm not aware of having any hostility toward people of color or feeling any superiority over them. I think if I felt such things, I would know it.

5. If I have racist thoughts or feelings, then I want to know it. I'll keep asking God to show me if I do and to have the humility to admit it. But I can't, with any integrity, tell you I'm racist just to appease you. I'm sure you don't want to be patronized, and I don't want to be dishonest.

"Whether you are hostile to people of color or not, you enjoy white privilege. You don't know what it's like to be pulled over by police because of your race, or denied credit, or viewed suspiciously, or passed over in employment. You're privileged, so you're complicit in systemic racism."

1. If we disagree on some points, don't assume that means I don't want to know what your life, or the life of any person of color, has been like. I do want to know. It does matter to me. And if there are injustices you still experience, I want to know what I can do about them.

2. I agree that whites can never fully understand what minorities experience. That does not make me racist, but it does make me ignorant of what racial minorities have experienced, which is something I do want to better understand.

3. I agree that being in the majority always carries some benefit. Majority members will always see more representation of themselves and will seldom know the discomfort of being in a minority. That's not racism, it's the unavoidable reality of any group. The question is whether the minority is receiving unfair treatment or the majority is receiving preferential treatment. Those are the moral wrongs that need to be righted.

"Racism is a systemic problem, not just an individual one. You don't have to be personally biased to be part of the problem."

1. *Systemic* means part of the overall system, which may be true

but hard to locate. Can we get more specific as to where the problem shows up? If we can't locate it, then we can't solve it.

2. If the problem is with a specific organization or institution, then let's focus on that organization or institution, specify the charges against it, and address each charge on its own merits. But if we just say, "It's everywhere," then we can't get anywhere.

3. If the problem is with an individual or group, then let's focus on that individual or group, specify the charges against them, and address each charge on its own merits. But again, if we just say, "It's everywhere," then we can't get anywhere.

"That sounds like a lot of Whitesplaining."

1. That term's a little vague. Can you explain what it means to you?

2. If I tried to explain to you what your own experience is, then sure, the term *Whitesplaining* applies. No white person can tell a person of color what it's like to be a person of color.

3. If I disagree with your conclusions or your positions, I am not discounting your experience, so that's not Whitesplaining.

4. As a man, I could never know what it's like to be a woman in a crisis pregnancy. But if her conclusion is that she should have an abortion, then I will disagree. That does not discount her story, but it challenges her conclusion. The same is true here. I cannot know what your experience with white people has been like. But if you conclude from your experience that all whites are racist, then I will disagree with your conclusion without invalidating your experience.

5. If Whitesplaining refers to whites trying to explain what people of color experience, then I think the term is fair. If

it's applied to any white person's comments or opinions about race, then I think the term is being used unfairly and inaccurately.

"Your resistance to admitting your white privilege is evidence of white fragility."

1. If by white privilege you mean that my color has not made life harder for me, but your color has, at times, made life harder for you, then I think the term *white privilege* applies.

2. If by white privilege you mean to say my life is essentially more privileged than yours, then I disagree. How can you know that? In which ways have I been more privileged than you, and in which ways have you been more privileged than I? You don't know everything about my past, you don't know everything about my present, you don't know how privileged or hard my life has been, and you don't know how privileged or hard my life is now. You don't know these things about me, and I don't know these things about you. So neither of us is in a position to label the other. Let's get to know each other before we say who's got more privilege.

3. Disagreement is not white fragility, it's human ability. We all have the ability to hear, assess, and form an opinion. That's what I've done, which has nothing to do with fragility.

4. Feeling defensive or making a verbal defense isn't fragility. When anyone is accused, they'll feel defensive. That's about being human, not being white. Anyone who's accused will want to respond. That's a human quality too, not a racial one. Judge my defense by what I'm saying, not by the fact that I'm saying it nor by the way I feel when I do.

"Since you're part of the hegemonic structure, you're not qualified to speak to racial issues. You should listen, not talk."

1. Since *hegemonic* means "ruling or dominant," I don't think a person's color automatically makes them part of that structure. There are people of color in much higher positions of influence and power than I, and white people in much lower positions of influence and power than you.

2. I am part of the majority race, so yes, I should listen to the stories of people of color who've had experiences I haven't had. I should weep or rejoice with people who are weeping or rejoicing.

3. Since racism is something affecting all of us, then all of us need to talk about it. We all need to be part of the discussion about what it is, where it is, and how to combat it. If we won't address the problem together, we can hardly expect to find a solution together.

"Your ancestors enslaved African people, and now you're getting the benefits of their labor. You need to pay."

1. There's no way slavery, segregation, and all the racist policies and ideas that supported them would not have some kind of effect on African-American families for generations.

2. There's no way to measure that effect today because African-American families and individuals have been impacted by it in different ways and to different extents over the past two centuries.

3. Reparations to other groups in the past have been made to the people directly damaged by a government's actions, or to their immediate offspring. At that point, damage can more fairly be identified and gauged. That is not the case when it comes to African-American slavery.

4. You don't know who my ancestors were, nor do I know who yours were. There were black slaves and white slave owners, but there were also black slave traders who sold black slaves, and there were white abolitionists who risked their lives to free them. For all we know, your ancestors may have contributed to the slave trade, and my ancestors may have fought against it.

5. Race does not determine ancestral behavior.

6. To some extent, all of us in today's America benefit from the slave labor of yesterday's America, regardless of our race. For that matter, all of us in modern civilization probably benefit, to some extent, from the slave labors of ancient civilizations. That is not a fault on our part, and it does not make us guilty of heinous sins committed centuries ago.

"You can't complain about me yelling at you or acting in ways you call 'inappropriate' because acting up is the only way to get white people to listen!"

1. I'll never complain about you being angry over mistreatment. Telling me you're angry is honest, but taking your anger out on me, whether by yelling or threatening or interfering with me, isn't fair or right. Unless I've done something directly to you, your anger over past injustice won't justify you being unjust toward me.

2. I want to listen to you, but not if it means being abused by you.

3. Acting up draws more attention to your rage than to the message you want people to hear. If you intimidate people into silence, that doesn't mean you've reached them.

4. The fact that someone doesn't agree with you doesn't mean they didn't hear you. I agree with some of what you've said,

and I disagree with some of what you've said, but I've heard all of what you've said.

"There may be some people of color who agree with you, but only because they've internalized the racism they've seen and heard all their lives."

1. If we say that we know why someone thinks the way they do, we're presuming to have powers we don't have. You and I cannot read minds, so we've got no business judging why someone believes what they believe.

2. It's possible some people internalize racism and wind up identifying with, then defending, racists. What's not possible is to know for certain who those people are based only on their beliefs about race.

3. I would never say that if someone believes in the critical race theory, it's only because they're a person of color or a social/political liberal. That isn't true, and it would be arrogant and presumptuous for me to say it. That works both ways.

4. One of the problems with racism is that it makes predetermined judgments about people. Let's not make that same mistake.

"Inequities in education access, housing, crime rates in neighborhoods, arrests, and incarcerations are all proof of systemic racism."

1. They may be the aftermath of past systemic racism, or the proof of present systemic racism, or a combination of the two.

2. If there is racism practiced within the system, it should be verifiable, brought to light, and corrected. As long as it is spoken of in generalities, none of those three can happen.

3. Situational differences between populations doesn't prove that racism alone, or even primarily, is the cause. The cause of the differences, not the differences themselves, is what needs to be proven.

"God cares about justice for the oppressed, so you should care too."

1. It's unfair and inaccurate to say that I don't care about the oppressed, just because I do not support the same policies and concepts that you do. We both care about the oppressed, but we have different views on who they are, what causes their oppression, and how to best help them.

2. When discrimination is proven to exist, it should be fought legally and socially. I will be a part of that fight.

3. Since I believe that sin is the ultimate problem, I also believe that the most important solution to offer is the remedy for sin found in the cross of Jesus Christ. So long as sin exists, its symptoms, such as racism, will exist as well.

4. Christianity promotes justice for the oppressed, justice for people accused of being oppressors, and fair treatment of both.

"White Christians supported slavery, just as white Christians supported segregation. So here you are, acting just like white Christians always have!"

1. Some white Christians supported slavery, and some white Christians supported segregation. That's horrendous, and it was a lethal doctrinal and moral error on their parts.

2. Many white Christians not only did not support slavery and segregation, but also actively opposed it, sometimes at great cost during the abolitionist movement and the civil rights movement.

3. It's not logical or just to say that because some people within a group committed an error in the past, all people in that same group must be committing the same error in the present.

"You will never understand what it's like to be a person of color."

1. Never, and that's one reason I'm glad we're talking. I know people of color have suffered more than I realize, and I want to hear their stories, grieve with them, be a friend and ally, and take actions that are fair and redemptive.

2. The fact that I can't fully understand your experience disqualifies me from ever saying, "I know just what you're going through."

3. The fact that I can't fully understand your experience does not disqualify me from having an informed opinion on how we should respond to the problem of racism. There are many hard experiences people of all kinds have had—abuse, poverty, serious illness—that I may not relate to, but I'm still capable of approving or rejecting ideas on what should be done for the people who've had those experiences.

"There's no point in talking to you. You'll always be racist. Even if you admitted it, you'd never fully get over it. It's a permanent disease."

1. If I don't accept your narrative, that doesn't mean our conversation is pointless. I appreciate you taking time to talk about this, and I wish you wouldn't give up on our conversation just because of our ongoing disagreement.

2. Please reconsider ending a conversation just because you didn't persuade someone to accept all your arguments. You and I probably agree on more things than we disagree on, and we could find common ground and build on that.

3. I still want to talk, even if you want to discontinue for now. Please keep that in mind.

4. I'm not convinced I'm a racist, but I will always be a sinner in need of God's grace. That's something I will, as you said, never fully get over.

> *"This is a world of compensations; and he who would*
> *be no slave, must consent to have no slave. Those who*
> *deny freedom to others, deserve it not for themselves;*
> *and, under a just God, cannot long retain it."*
>
> ABRAHAM LINCOLN

CHAPTER NINE

MY BODY VS. MY SELF

Discussing Transgender

This is an unexpected conversation. Most of us never thought we'd discuss the transgender issue, first, because we knew so little about it, second, because we doubted we'd ever know a transgender person, and third, because the facts about our sexes seemed so self-evident, we didn't think they'd be challenged.

All that's changed with breathtaking speed over the past decade, forcing Christians to confront cultural shifts and, in many cases, upheaval within their own families.

It's common knowledge today that the transgender movement is closely aligned with the gay rights movement, hence the popular label LGBTQ (lesbian, gay, bisexual, transgender, queer). The transgender movement has drawn generously from the playbook of the gay rights movement.

From the seventies onward, gay acceptance was advanced through films, television characters, sympathetic journalists, the American Psychiatric Association, anti-discrimination laws, the educational system, and celebrities "coming out."

The national debate shifted accordingly, the question eventually evolving from "Is homosexuality normal?" to "Are *objections* to homosexuality normal?" Those who hold such objections now find themselves subject to intense pressure and scorn.

That movement's success is now emulated by its transsexual cousin, which has also advanced itself through films (*The Danish Girl*; *Boys Don't Cry*), television shows (*Orange Is the New Black*; *POSE*; *The Good Doctor*), sympathetic journalists (Barbara Walters, "My Secret Self," 2007; Anderson Cooper, "Transgender Former Navy Seal Speaks Out," 2017), the American Psychiatric Association (change in diagnostic status from "gender identity disorder" to "gender dysphoria"), antidiscrimination laws (the Equality Act), and the education system (Title IX interpreted to allow transgender persons to participate in sports).

The celebrity factor has also helped, with figures such as Olympian Bruce Jenner (aka Caitlyn Jenner) and actress Ellen Page (aka Elliot Page) publicly reidentifying from one sex to another.

As before, the national debate has shifted accordingly, with 62 percent of Americans saying they've become more supportive of transgender rights in the last five years.[1] The question, "Is transgender normal?" has also shifted to, "Are objections to transgender normal?" and, in some cases, "Should objections even be allowed?" As of this writing, for example, Norway has passed a bill outlawing private remarks against transgenderism, the penalty being up to a year in prison.[2]

Predictably, as the option to dis-identify with one's birth sex became acceptable, people who wouldn't have chosen that option in the past are choosing it now. Statistics from 2016 showed 1.4 million Americans identifying as transgender, nearly double the number who identified as such ten years earlier,[3] leaving a growing number of people (many of them Christian) hearing a loved one say, "Mom, Dad, I'm a nonbinary transgender."

TERMS AND CONCEPTS

Before discussing a response, let's clarify the terms associated with the word *transgender*, the umbrella label for subgroups such as transsexuals, drag queens, and transvestites.

Transsexual was the diagnostic term previously used for individuals who felt more identified with the opposite sex than their birth sex. The word indicated those feelings were pathological, which many transsexuals found offensive. Similar to the way gays lobbied to have homosexuality reclassified (from disorder to normal) by the American Psychiatric Association in 1973, so trans activists are making similar advances.

In the most recent revision of the *Diagnostic and Statistical Manuel for Mental and Emotional Disorders* (the DSM-5), the term *transsexual* has been replaced with *gender dysphoria*, which lists the distress a trans person may feel as being the problem, rather than the transsexualism itself.[4]

Currently, then, the term *gender dysphoric* is used instead of *transsexual* to reference a person who feels trapped in the wrong body. A person who is gender dysphoric may be attracted to the opposite sex or to the same sex, so it's a mistake to assume such a person is a gay man who wants to become a woman or a lesbian woman who wants to become a man. In many cases, the person may want to live as the opposite sex while still being attracted to, and partnering with, the opposite sex.

A *transvestite*, in contrast, is someone who enjoys wearing clothing of the opposite sex without a wish to become the opposite sex. Transvestites are often though not always heterosexual, dressing as the opposite sex for sexual and emotional pleasure.

Female impersonators (commonly called *drag queens*) rarely qualify as transsexuals or gender dysphorics since they live as men, assuming their female persona episodically, not permanently. Most homosexuals have no desire to change their sex, so they, too, are distinct from transsexuals.

The groups *queer* and *nonbinary* are both vague. Queer refers to just about any appearance, behavior, or mentality outside the gender mainstream. Nonbinary means not in conformity to standard male/female identification. Both terms are fluid and used interchangeably.

All subgroups—transsexuals/gender dysphorics, drag queens, transvestites, queer, and nonbinary—get lumped together under the term *transgender*. More often than not, though, you'll find the transgender person is gender dysphoric.

A discussion about this topic will usually include three subtopics: innateness, irrelevance, and inevitability.

INBORN AND UNCHANGEABLE:
THE INNATENESS ARGUMENT

Many transgender individuals feel, from early in life, "trapped" in the wrong body, so the American Psychiatric Association's definition of transsexualism was "strong and persistent cross-gender identification... and...persistent discomfort about one's assigned sex."[5]

But it's also common for transsexuals to develop the depression of gender dysphoria, a torment expressing itself in the question, "How can I be one way yet feel another?" No one should dismiss the seriousness of this depression because suicide attempts, drug abuse, and horrendous efforts at self-mutilation are commonly reported among young transgenders.[6]

The modern solution, often advised and celebrated, is a process called *transitioning*. It can be as minor as a change of clothing and appearance or as significant as gender affirmation surgery, through which the transgender's body is altered to conform to his or her self-perception.

The desired sex is the target, as opposed to the sex he or she was born with. Transitioning or gender affirmation surgery can include injections of hormones, facial reconstruction, breast implants or removal, and reconstruction of genitals.

This process is widely available, even at times to children, although most states require a person to live (dress, work, and self-identify) as a member of the opposite sex for a prescribed period before undergoing surgery, accompanied by psychological counseling to determine suitability for the procedure.

The impossibility of literally becoming the opposite sex seems obvious, but so does the desperation a person must feel to make such an attempt. Surely castration, implants, and hormones still leave a man unable to ovulate; penile implants and breast reduction likewise won't delete a woman's womanhood. Chromosomes stubbornly remain unchanged, immune to surgical intervention. Plainly put, body parts can be changed but DNA cannot.

Knowing all this and more, thousands still attempt reassignment, believing that they were born not for the body they inhabit but for the one they're trying to create. In this attempt, they're getting unprecedented support.

Until recently, the testimony of the body overrode the mind. If a man felt like a woman yet inhabited a male body, his feelings, not his body, were viewed as the problem. They were considered something to be resisted, modified if possible, and contrary to what is.

Currently, what one *is* is being determined by what one *feels*—an ominous trend when the implications are considered. It is, in essence, an attempt to define reality by desire, knowledge by intuition.

Transsexualism's increased acceptance, combined with its early developmental appearance, leaves many professionals and laity assuming that it is an inborn trait. The jury, after all, is still out on the question of homosexuality's origins—inborn, acquired, or a combination of the two?—and compelling arguments are made on all sides. Biological or genetic factors may also create, or at least contribute to, this mystery as well.

Yet not only has transsexualism not been proven to be inborn, the theories proposed to explain its origins are strikingly similar to those currently proposed to explain homosexuality. The Bioethics Observatory Institute of Life Science has this to say: "In summary, the factors that cause transsexualism remain unknown, although it appears most likely to be the result of the interaction of multiple factors: biological, psychological and social."[7]

Like homosexuality, the experience of the transgender person is usually involuntary, a case in which a person feels something unasked for but deeply ingrained. That alone can make it seem like an inborn condition, but as of this writing, the proof isn't there.

WE ARE WHO WE ARE, REGARDLESS: THE IRRELEVANCE ARGUMENT

"You talk about sex reassignment as though God's against it, but does it really matter to Him what sex we are?" I was once asked by an angry transgender person. Pointing to the Bible on my desk, he said,

"I've read in the New Testament that in Christ, we're neither male nor female. If that's true, then God's not even looking at my gender!"

I reached for the Bible and nodded. "You're quoting from Galatians 3:28. Let me read it. 'There is neither Jew nor Greek, there is neither slave nor free, there is neither male nor female; for you are all one in Christ Jesus.'"

"Seems pretty clear to me," he responded.

"But remember the context," I said. "Paul's talking about justification, and he begins the paragraph by saying, 'For you are all sons of God through faith in Christ Jesus.' He means whatever our race, sex, or status, we're all one in Christ. But he didn't say race and sex have disappeared; he simply said they don't affect our standing before God."

He shook his head. "I don't know about that. I think God cares more about my character than my sex. I'm a decent person, I'm not hurting anyone, and I'm living a responsible life. I can't see God caring about something as irrelevant as my body parts."

It's an understandable argument, borrowing from Martin Luther King Jr.'s famous speech in which he envisioned a world where children are judged, not by the color of their skin, but by the content of their character.

Stretching the point further than King intended, some argue that since the importance of one's sex pales in comparison to one's character, sex is a trait one can change at will. One's assigned sex is relegated to an optional status, alongside hair color or body weight, both of which can be changed at our discretion and neither of which is primary to God.

This is problematic at several levels.

First, separating sex from character requires a dualism of body versus soul, rather than the value of body, soul, and spirit described in Scripture. The first assignments of sex in history were divinely commanded and commended. In Genesis 1:27, humanity is created in God's image and defined by sex ("in the image of God He created them male and female"). Further, God applauds His handiwork when He pronounces it "very good" (Genesis 1:31). The male/female complement is thereby God-ordained, expressive of both human need and divine nature. That alone tells us that one's biological sex is hardly secondary.

Second, our sex is designated with God's foreknowledge. Examples abound of instances when God or His messengers foretold the sex of a forthcoming child (Genesis 18:10; Judges 13:3; Luke 1:31). And His foreordination in shaping individual traits, gender included, is confirmed to Jeremiah, "Before I formed you in the womb I knew you" (Jeremiah 1:5), and by David,

> For You formed my inward parts;
> You covered me in my mother's womb.
> I will praise You, for I am fearfully and wonderfully made.
> (Psalm 139:13-14)

Our sex, then, is neither accidental nor irrelevant. It's a critical distinctive, endowed on each of us with God's knowledge and by His plan, since our bodies are in part our selves, and we, in our entirety, were foreknown and foreordained.

REVISITING GNOSTICISM

Perhaps the broader and greater error of transgender advocates is a denigration of the body as being subject to the whims of its owner. In this sense, transsexualism hearkens to the ancient heresy of Gnosticism, which dates back to the first century and was so despised by John and Paul in their epistles and still, under different names and guises, plagues us today.

Gnostic belief dictates that humanity's imperfection is the fault of an imperfect creator, referred to as the demiurge, who was himself an inferior emanation of God crudely comparable to the devil.[8]

The body, to the Gnostic, is but one of the demiurge's many flawed creations, and its inhabitants the "divine souls trapped in a material world created by an imperfect spirit." Whereas the Bible views the body as good and preordained, Gnosticism views it as inherently bad, creating the Gnostic belief that Jesus was only a spirit who wouldn't have inhabited an evil body, countered by John's statement that "every spirit that does not confess that Jesus Christ has come in the flesh is not of God" (1 John 4:3).

If the body is essentially evil, created by Someone who got it wrong, then it is up to the individual to determine the use and purpose of the body. Gnostics, in fact, encourage reliance on intuition (what one feels) in contrast to what is physically clear, describing their practice as "the knowledge of transcendence arrived at by way of *internal, intuitive means*" (emphasis added).[9]

The created, not the Creator, has the final say based on his or her sense of right and wrong, so the "basis of action is the moral inclination of the individual"[10]

Consider all of this in light of what transgenders often say: "I identify as a woman/man, so I am one!" an assurance Gnosticism says is "arrived at by way of internal, intuitive means" with "the moral inclination of the individual" being the basis of action.

"But you're forgetting your own argument," my transgender friend interrupted when I pointed this out. "You said we're a fallen race, so we could have inborn traits God never meant us to have, right?"

"If those traits contradict what He intended, yes," I said.

"So who's to say my sex isn't a birth defect? You said we're born imperfect because of the sin nature. What if God intended me to be a woman, but because of fallen nature—birth defect, as you say—I was born a man? If that's the case, shouldn't I correct what was wrong to begin with?"

"If the thing is wrong in and of itself, I could see that," I agreed. "If you're born without a leg, a prosthetic device makes sense. If you have an inborn chemical imbalance, there's no reason you shouldn't correct it through medication."

"That goes for my body parts too," he said.

"Not the same thing. If something is inherently wrong, it's a flaw. But being male or female isn't a handicap or a sinful tendency. We can only call something a flaw if it's defective in and of itself. Otherwise, if something inherently natural about our body is at odds with our desires, then our desires are the problem, not vice versa."

We have a Creator whose will is revealed in an inspired document (2 Timothy 3:16). That document testifies to gender's relevance by describing:

- The foreordained assignment of each person's sex (Jeremiah 1:5; Psalm 139:13-14)

- The interdependence between the sexes (Genesis 2:18,21-24)

- Distinct gender roles, attributes, and responsibilities (Proverbs 14:1; 1 Corinthians 11:3-15; Ephesians 5:22-33; 1 Timothy 2:8-15; 5:8)

Common sense testifies to created intent as well. People are born male or female, a distinction marking the first words referring to them as "It's a boy!" or "It's a girl!" Saying that one feels like something else doesn't make it so. Reassignment surgery, likewise, changes the body but not the sex, constituting, as apologist Greg Bahnsen says, "a bizarre biological masquerade."[11]

As for irrelevance, our character and gender are separate, but they are both critical. Our manhood or womanhood is not a suggestion to be accepted or discarded. It is an unalterable assignment, mandated by a Creator who both intended and designed it for the individual to whom He entrusted it.

Oliver O'Donovan, professor of moral and pastoral theology at the University of Oxnard, emphasizes this when he asserts: "If I claim to have a 'real sex' which may be at war with the sex of my body and is at least in a rather uncertain relationship to it, I am shrinking from the glad acceptance of myself as a physical as well as a spiritual being, and seeking self-knowledge in a kind of Gnostic withdrawal from material creation."[12]

I HAVE TO CHANGE TO BE ME: THE INEVITABILITY ARGUMENT

Defaulting to the conviction that one is trapped in the wrong body is often presented as the answer to the conflict, but this seems to be a premature assumption.

Dr. Paul McHugh, the university-distinguished service professor of psychiatry at the Johns Hopkins University School of Medicine, explains why: "Transgendered men do not become women, nor do transgendered women become men. All (including Bruce Jenner) become feminized men or masculinized women, counterfeits or impersonators of the sex with which they 'identify.' In that lies their problematic future."[13]

The "problematic future" McHugh cites includes more than disappointment in the lack of resolution gender-affirmation surgery may bring. There can also be long-term, serious consequences to such an extraordinary attempt to change the unchangeable.

According to Dr. Ryan T. Anderson, senior research fellow at the Heritage Foundation, a thirty-year follow up of sex-reassigned people found a "lifelong mental unrest" among the subjects.[14] "Ten to 15 years after surgical reassignment, the suicide rate of those who had undergone sex-reassignment surgery rose to 20 times that of comparable peers."[15]

Furthermore, a meta-analysis of over one hundred follow-up studies on postoperative transsexuals concluded that "none of the studies provides conclusive evidence that gender reassignment is beneficial for patients."[16] The 2016 "Proposed Decision Memo for Gender Dysphoria and Gender Reassignment Surgery" agreed, stating, "there is not enough evidence to determine whether gender reassignment surgery improves health outcomes for Medicare beneficiaries with gender dysphoria."[17] And the Obama Centers for Medicare and Medicaid Services pointed out a "19-times-greater likelihood for death by suicide, and a host of other poor outcomes."[18]

We should empathize deeply with anyone in anguish over a disconnect between the body they inhabit and the body they want. We can approach that person with respect for their struggle while still feeling heartache should they attempt to resolve it by transitioning. Our heartache is grounded in the firm belief their creator established something they are, in futility, trying to reverse.

Dr. Michelle Cretella, the president of the American College of Pediatricians, elaborates on this: "The norm for human development is for one's thoughts to align with physical reality, and for one's gender identity to align with one's biologic sex."[19]

Or as God affirmed to Peter in the book of Acts: "What God has cleansed you must not call common" (Acts 10:15).

KEEP IN MIND

The following general points are significant when considering transgender individuals from a biblical worldview.

1. The typical transgender person has wrestled privately and fiercely with the decision to transition. Show you respect that struggle by asking about his or her life experience, listening carefully, and showing compassion without condoning the proposed solution.

2. To the transgender person who feels transitioning is the only option and is trying to be at peace with that, your disagreement can be seen as a threat to her or his peace of mind.

3. To attempt a transition from one sex to another is to usurp divine authority and attempt to call things that are not as though they are.

4. You can and should empathize with another person's pain. You cannot align yourself with another person's falsehood.

5. It is impossible to become the opposite sex. It is possible only to make your body resemble the opposite sex.

KEEP IT BIBLICAL

The following general points are significant when examining transgender persons from a biblical worldview.

1. God established the binary of male and female from the beginning, with no third option.

   So God created man in His own image; in the image

of God He created him; male and female He created them (Genesis 1:27).

And He answered and said to them, "Have you not read that He who made them at the beginning 'made them male and female'" (Matthew 19:4).

2. The sex we are born with is foreknown and foreordained by God.

> "Before I formed you in the womb I knew you;
> Before you were born I sanctified you;
> I ordained you a prophet to the nations."
> (Jeremiah 1:5)

> For You formed my inward parts;
> You covered me in my mother's womb.
> I will praise You, for I am fearfully and wonderfully made;
> Marvelous are Your works,
> And that my soul knows very well.
> My frame was not hidden from You,
> When I was made in secret,
> And skillfully wrought in the lowest parts of the earth.
> Your eyes saw my substance, being yet unformed.
> And in Your book they all were written,
> The days fashioned for me,
> When as yet there were none of them.
> (Psalm 139:13-16)

3. The only reference to adopting the dress of the opposite sex is negative.

> "A woman shall not wear anything that pertains to a man, nor shall a man put on a woman's garment, for all who do so are an abomination to the LORD your God" (Deuteronomy 22:5).

4. It's foolish for the created being to question the wisdom of her or his Creator.

> Surely you have things turned around!
> Shall the potter be esteemed as the clay;
> For shall the thing made say of him who made it,
> "He did not make me"?
> Or shall the thing formed say of him who formed it,
> "He has no understanding"?
> (Isaiah 29:16)

5. It's destructive for the created being to strive against the intentions of her or his Creator.

> "Woe to him who strives with his Maker!
> Let the potsherd strive with the potsherds of the earth!
> Shall the clay say to him who forms it,
> 'What are you making?'
> Or shall your handiwork say, 'He has no hands'?"
> (Isaiah 45:9)

KEEP IT GOING

The following are some of the questions or arguments you're likely to hear when discussing transgenderism, along with some suggested points for keeping the discussion going.

"I've always felt I was in the wrong body."

1. It's got to be tormenting to feel that way. What was it like for you? How did you handle it? What did you think it meant?

2. If you feel you're in the wrong body, couldn't the problem be the feeling, not the body?

3. If we have a Creator, and He made you the sex you are, do you really think He got it wrong?

"Do you think for a minute I chose to feel this way?"

1. Not at all. Who would choose a conflict like this?

2. We've all got feelings or conflicts we didn't choose. Some of us have challenges through no choice or fault of our own that are pretty big. This is one of them.

3. I won't pretend I know what this is like, but I know you didn't choose to feel this way or make it happen.

"I'm a perfectly healthy person. This is the only thing that makes me different."

1. I agree, plenty of trans people are basically healthy, high-functioning people.

2. In fairness, healthy people can have an unhealthy quality but still be essentially healthy.

3. I don't think gender dysphoria is healthy. I think you are generally healthy. The one doesn't cancel out the other.

"The only problem transgenders have is the transphobia all around them."

1. There's prejudice against transgenders, for sure, meaning there are people who think you are less valuable than they are, and that mistreating you is OK. I'm not sure I'd call that a phobia, but I'm as against that as you are.

2. Is it fair to say that if someone disapproves of transitioning that makes them "phobic"? Wouldn't it be more accurate to say they have a different view?

3. You didn't choose this, but you are choosing how to respond

to it. Some will agree with your decision, some won't. Disagreement is neither a prejudice nor a phobia.

"I feel at peace since I've started transitioning, so it must be right."

1. You have the right to transition if that's what you feel will give you peace of mind.

2. Respectfully, though, is "feeling peace" the best way to decide on this? If you are trying to be something you really can't be, aren't the facts involved more important than the peace involved?

3. Is it possible you're mistaking temporary relief for genuine peace?

"I need you to be happy for me, because I've found myself."

1. I can love and value you, no problem. But is it fair to ask me to be happy about something I don't agree with?

2. This is your decision. But if you're asking me to agree that you've found yourself, I can't. When the physical facts say you are one thing, and you say you've found yourself to be something else, I have to believe the physical facts.

"I need you to call me by my preferred name and pronoun."

1. I never want to offend you, so I'll try to use words that don't needlessly offend. I can greet you without calling you a proper name and without using the name you don't want to be called by.

2. Please don't ask me to call you by names and pronouns that represent something I don't believe is real. I won't impose on

you the names and pronouns you reject. Please don't impose words on me that I can't affirm.

"Lack of acceptance from people like you drives trans people to depression and suicide."

1. Lack of acceptance hurts people, for sure. But I do accept you. I care about you, value you, and want you in my life.

2. Acceptance and agreement are two different things. You're wrong if you think my lack of agreement on this issue is also a lack of acceptance. If I didn't accept you, we wouldn't be talking.

3. The suicide rate among trans people is higher than the general population, even among transgenders who have a community of support around them. Clearly, something other than lack of acceptance plays into this.

"If we deny children and teens the right to transition, we cause them harm."

1. Plenty of children and teens who identify as trans early in life outgrow that identification. It doesn't help to prematurely encourage a label that may not stick.

2. The decision to transition should be a fully informed decision made by an adult. The ramifications for transitioning are too serious for this to be decided on before adulthood.

3. Trans kids are not harmed by delaying the transition process. They are harmed by people rejecting, abusing, or humiliating them, but they're not harmed by delaying such a permanent, life-altering choice.

"I'm still me, whether I'm a woman or a man."

1. Being who you are includes being the sex you were born. I believe your sex is assigned before birth and is an innate part of who you are. So if you're still you, I believe that means you're still who and what you were born.

2. I get your point—you're still essentially the same personality as before. I agree with that and still value you no matter how you identify.

3. But in fairness, you can't expect me to jump into seeing you as another sex when I've always known you as one sex and still believe you are that sex. I think you are still you, the same you I've always known.

"The Bible says there is neither male nor female in Christ, so obviously whatever sex we choose isn't important."

1. That verse—Galatians 3:28—doesn't say the male/female distinctions don't exist. It only says they have nothing to do with our position in Christ, which is available to everyone.

2. God determines our sex before we're formed in the womb. When it comes to our value and access to Him, that sex becomes irrelevant but never nonexistent.

"Trans people are always happier when they embrace who they really are."

1. Technically I agree, because I believe trans people are the sex they were born with and will be happier if they embrace who they really are.

2. I know you mean they are happier if they transition. But

statistics show transitioning often doesn't bring the happiness it was expected to bring.

"If this is who I am, and God created me, then God created me trans."

1. God doesn't create a conflict between us and our own bodies. We are shaped by design and with intention.

2. Because we're a fallen race, we're beset with lots of conflict God never created or intended.

"If I say I am a male or a female, then that's what I am because that's how I identify."

1. We can't speak things into existence. We can identify with something, but that alone doesn't make it real.

2. Only God has the authority and power to speak into existence what is not. Attempting to do that, as humans, is a way of usurping divine authority.

"If you can't accept me for who I am, then I have to keep my distance from you. I won't tolerate someone who's transphobic."

1. I was hoping this wouldn't come between us. It doesn't have to. People disagree and still relate. Can't we?

2. Help me understand how you define transphobic. If I think something's wrong, does that really make me "phobic"?

3. If you think I'm wrong about transgenders, that's fair. But unless I treat you with disrespect or hostility, I really think the transphobic label is way off base.

4. If you withdraw from me because of this, I won't withdraw

from you. As far as I'm concerned, our relationship is more important than our differences. I will always feel that way, and I hope that someday you will too.

"When we want to be something other than the thing God wants us to be, we must be wanting what, in fact, will not make us happy."

C.S. Lewis

CHAPTER TEN

AN ORGY OF VIRTUE

*Discussing Sin, Salvation,
and Progressive Christianity*

U rgency is a running theme in the book of Acts. Luke's account of the early church describes people entrusted with an urgent message, propelled by the urgency of eternal issues to get that message out and to keep the main things the main things.

Those main things included a conviction people were lost because of sin: "Repent, and let every one of you be baptized in the name of Jesus Christ for the remission of sins" (Acts 2:38).

If lost, they were headed for judgment: "Because He has appointed a day on which He will judge the world in righteousness by the Man whom He has ordained" (Acts 17:31).

The only solution was reconciliation to God through faith in Christ, who alone had made the acceptable sacrifice for sin: "For there is no other name under heaven given among men by which we must be saved" (Acts 4:12).

The early believers knew those three points—man's sinfulness, the coming judgment, and Christ as the only way of salvation—were essential. Relentless persecutions never shook them off that doctrinal tripod.

Remove or dilute these three essentials, and you have nothing left of the gospel. If humanity is not inherently sinful, then nobody's sick; don't call the doctor (Mark 2:17). If Jesus is not the only way to the Father as He claimed to be (John 14:6), then there's no need for evangelism. If there's no coming judgment, there's no need to examine our ways, so eat and drink, for tomorrow we die (1 Corinthians 15:32). Under these terms the cross makes no sense nor, for that matter, does most of the New Testament.

Yet the rejection of and opposition to these doctrines comes less from secular opponents and more from professing believers. While many nonbelievers find them offensive, those doctrines are more in danger of being dismantled by progressive Christians than by the Cancel Culture.

That is not to say secular influences don't come into play here. Most likely they provided a template of thought and approach for progressive Christians, who seem to have adopted social trends and baptized them in religious terms.

First, the template. A cluster of groups has claimed the high moral ground, demanding the rest of us convert or cower before them. The woke generation, those "aware of and actively attentive to important facts and issues";[1] Cancel Culture, those withdrawing support or cancelling people or groups they find offensive;[2] the social justice warriors righting wrongs;[3] and the radical Black Lives Matter and Antifa movements combine to stage an orgy of virtue celebrating their interpretation of justice and, quite unabashedly, their own righteousness.

To these groups, binaries such as male/female are anathema. Traditional sexual mores are bigotry. Traditional evangelism is thinly disguised nationalism. The larger issues they believe we all should address include social justice, ending racism, slowing global warming, redistributing wealth, and ending all vestiges of oppression. Enlightened people are expected to follow their lead in pursuing these goals above all others.

While some believers find all this a bit silly, a significant number of younger Christians, raised in orthodox homes but withdrawing from orthodox churches, are susceptible to these ideals, finding them an attractive answer to their need for meaning, a need they've decided the local church can no longer meet.[4]

To them, the commitment of these groups, the good they profess to do, and the social evils they fight meet two needs I believe all people, the young in particular, deeply feel: the need for passion and the need for a just cause.

I remember feeling those needs in high school when I first studied World War II and learned the specifics of the Holocaust. The bravery of the resistance fighters captured my imagination, and I felt jealous of women and men who'd put their lives on the line to rescue Jewish families in the face of national monstrosities. *How wonderful*, I thought, *to have something truly evil to fight, someone truly innocent to defend, and the passion to do both.* I wasn't just inspired, I was envious.

Lutheran pastor Hans Fiene called this dynamic "Selma envy," a reference to the effect studying Dr. King's marches on Selma during the civil rights movement had on him and his classmates:

> More than we wanted to find the perfect prom date, we wanted to find our own bigotry to eradicate. After years of hearing those saints sing "We Shall Overcome," we were overcome with jealousy. We coveted Selma. We envied that march. We looked at that footage and hungered for our own cause to devour.[5]

Columnist Andrew Sullivan elaborates on this vividly in a piece for *New York* magazine:

> For many, especially the young, discovering a new meaning in the midst of the fallen world is thrilling. And social-justice ideology does everything a religion should. It offers an account of the whole: that human life and society and any kind of truth must be seen entirely as a function of social power structures, in which various groups have spent all of human existence oppressing other groups. And it provides a set of practices to resist and reverse this interlocking web of oppression—from regulating the workplace and

policing the classroom to checking your own sin and even seeking to control language itself. I think of non-PC gaffes as the equivalent of old swear words. Like the Puritans, who were agape when someone used God's name in a curse, the new faithful are scandalized when someone says something "problematic." Another commonality of the zealot then and now: humorlessness.[6]

No wonder Cancel Culture attracts so many novitiates! It's all there: evil to fight, victims to protect, sinners to punish. Sadly, the times being so intellectually lazy, these converts storm the altar to embrace causes powered by half-truths and manipulations, but no matter. It may be bogus, but the cause is, as Sullivan noted, "thrilling."

Young Christians with diminished allegiance to their churches can be as susceptible as their secular counterparts, looking for ways to frame social justice campaigns in terms Christian enough to satisfy their upbringing but hip enough to satisfy their crusader instincts. Which may be why progressive influencer Rob Bell said, "I have long wondered if there is a massive shift coming in what it means to be a Christian. Something new is in the air."[7]

PROGRESSING TOWARD WHAT?

Enter the Christian progressives, providing a fresh approach to the faith complete with new priorities and righteous goals, answering the need for a cause without sacrificing Christian identity. A diversity of leaders and influencers communicate as progressive Christians, making a detailed account of their beliefs difficult. But the website *Progressive Christianity* has given us some points to clarify the contrast between progressive and orthodox Christianity:[8]

On salvation:

> [We] believe that following the path of the teacher Jesus can lead to healing and wholeness, a mystical connection to 'God,' as well as an awareness and experience of not only the Sacred, but the Oneness and Unity of all life."

On Jesus as the only way:

> [We] affirm that the teachings of Jesus provide but one of
> many ways to experience "God."

In believing Jesus is not *the* Way but one of many, progressive Christians share the views of the presiding bishop of the Episcopal Church who states, "We who practice the Christian tradition understand him (Jesus) as our vehicle to the divine. But for us to assume that God could not act in other ways is, I think, to put God in an awfully small box."[9] Professing (and clearly progressive) Christian Oprah Winfrey concurs: "There are millions of ways to God."[10]

On church fellowship:

> [We] seek and create community that is inclusive of ALL
> people, including but not limited to:...agnostics...those
> of all sexual orientations and all gender identities...all crea-
> tures and plant life.

On discipleship and Christian living:

> [We] know that the way we behave toward one another
> and Earth is the fullest expression of what we believe, there-
> fore we vow to walk as Jesus might have walked in this
> world with radical compassion, inclusion, and bravery to
> confront and positively change the injustices we experience
> as well as those we see others experiencing.

Other writings explain their take on the Bible's role and authority:

> While divinely inspired, we deny the Bible is inerrant or
> infallible. It was written by men over centuries and thus
> reflects both God's truth and human sin and prejudice. We
> affirm that Biblical scholarship and critical theory help us
> discern which messages are God's.[11]

Self-identified progressive Christian youth minister Anna Skate explains the progressive take on the doctrine of fallen human nature:

> There is nothing inherent to these children's humanity from which they need to be saved. Therefore, an atonement theology of inborn corruption in need of redemption has no place in a conversation with kids about Easter.[12]

She also elaborates on the doctrine of hell, which she says, "suggests that God is a being sitting on some shiny throne literally evaluating every individual life from afar, casting judgement and glaring in disdain."[13]

Let's unpack this. Progressive Christians do not believe Jesus is the only way to salvation, nor that humanity is sinful, in need of being saved, and in danger of judgment. Discipleship is more about kindness, except when confronting social injustice. Homosexuality and transgenderism are celebrated, and the earth with its creatures and plant life are included in Christian community.

This is, to overstate the obvious, a belief system utterly foreign to sound doctrine, and it collapses under the most casual examination from a biblical worldview. Blogger Natasha Crain recognized this when she wrote:

> Progressive Christians don't like apologetics because it challenges them to think of biblical teachings in a category of objective truth—something we're not free to change just because we happen to "experience" it in varied ways. Two plus two equals four whether I experience difficulty with that or not.[14]

PRETTY POISON

The wrongness of the progressive Christian message, ranging from startling falsehoods to glaring heresies, is tempered by the sheen of its messengers. Smiling faces of attractive, winsome ladies such as Jen

Hatmaker and the late Rachel Held Evans; the handsome pro-gay ethicist David Gushee; the daringly audacious and highly articulate Rob Bell; the thunderous provocateur Tony Campolo; and recognized scholars such as Marcus Borg, Peter Enns, and Richard Beck all present a credible, inviting image. It's pretty poison served up as relevant Christianity, layers of error influencing believers hungry to fight for social justice and, in the process, neglects the urgent truths early and modern Christians shed blood for.

Its impact on congregations is well described by Alisa Childers, a specialist in examining and critiquing progressive Christianity. In her article "5 Signs Your Church Might Be Heading Toward Progressive Christianity,"[15] she cites a lowered view of the Bible, feelings emphasized over facts, essential Christian doctrines open to reinterpretation, historical terms redefined, and the heart of the gospel message shifting from sin and redemption to social justice as effects progressive Christianity has on churches who embrace it.

The church with a lowered view of Scripture and an elevated view of feelings, a high concern for social justice and low concern for evangelism, and a reinterpretation of basic doctrine and a rejection of historic concepts, is a church that cannot lead anyone from death to life, nor disciple and nurture those who are already alive. It's a church proud of its virtue, pharisaical in its smug rejection of sound doctrine in lieu of enlightenment. Look for it in vain in the book of Acts, but see it warned in the book of the Revelation:

> "I know your works, love, service, faith, and your patience; and as for your works, the last are more than the first. Nevertheless I have a few things against you, because you allow that woman Jezebel, who calls herself a prophetess, to teach and seduce My servants to commit sexual immorality and eat things sacrificed to idols. And I gave her time to repent of her sexual immorality, and she did not repent. Indeed I will cast her into a sickbed, and those who commit adultery with her into great tribulation, unless they repent of their deeds" (Revelation 2:19-22).

Yet when established, orthodox leaders like Max Lucado offer progressives like Jen Hatmaker the assurance that their differences are hardly worth quibbling over (see chapter 7), then credulous believers are left seeing these very errors Jesus warned against as incidental and those pointing them out as the problem. The irony is delicious: promote an attractive error and you're a good guy; correct it, and you're bad for doing so.

None of which jibes well with Scripture's approach to error in the church. Paul openly rebuked Peter's hypocrisy in distancing himself from Gentiles (Galatians 2:11-16). Paul called out Hymenaeus and Philetus for the cankerous effect their teaching had on churches (2 Timothy 2:16-18). John publicized his criticism of Diotrephes's love for preeminence (3 John 9). Paul lamented his knowledge that wolves would invade the Ephesian church (Acts 20:29). When it comes to false doctrine (and how else can we refer to progressive Christianity's tenets?), the Bible commends an attitude of lovingly fierce intolerance.

The reasons for this are quite practical. Within the church, the flock of believers is meant to be guided, nourished, corrected, and built up in the faith. That can't be done without direction to the right sources and sound concepts, so when voices within the church offer direction toward wrong sources, serious damage is done to sheep who are thereby led to eat all the wrong foods.

Look at it another way. An airplane usually has some food available on its flight. If a flight attendant gets a few items on the menu wrong when describing available snack items over the loudspeaker, no serious damage is done. That information is secondary.

The airplane also has oxygen masks to put on and exits to use in case of an emergency. If a flight attendant announces the wrong place to find a mask, or the wrong directions to the emergency exits, someone could die. That information is far from secondary, so there's no room for politeness. Someone will have to correct the message as a matter of life or death.

People coming to church need to be taught about the person and promises of Jesus Christ, the way to salvation, the warnings of judgment, the means of sanctification, the standards for godly living, and the promises and power available to them as joint heirs with Christ.

This information, too, is far from secondary. If somebody's sending the wrong message about these, someone else will have to correct the message as a matter of life and death.

No one was clearer than Jesus about the only way to the Father, the universal problem of sin, and the danger of hell. Anyone speaking into the church who confuses these essentials is indeed progressive because he or she is making progress toward a cliff and, in the process, drawing a following.

This is why the orgy of virtue posing as beauty needs to be exposed for its nakedness, and this is why we must again, as Jude advised, "contend earnestly for the faith which was once for all delivered to the saints" (Jude 3).

KEEP IN MIND

The following general points are significant when considering progressive Christianity from a biblical worldview.

1. The work of the church is the salvation of souls and the making of disciples. Other goals (such as charity and social justice) are important but secondary. When they are pursued at the expense of the essentials, or in ways contradictory to Scripture, then the church is in error.

2. If we are not clearly teaching that humanity is sinful and in need of salvation, that salvation is found only in Christ, and that the judgment of hell is real and to be feared, then we are not giving people the full and essential counsel of God.

3. Progressive Christianity is attractive in that it presents a cause, victims to protect, and enemies to resist.

4. We can and should admit that at times the church has shown indifference to critical social issues. We can correct the indifference without abdicating or minimizing the importance of sound doctrine.

5. When serious error is being publicly promoted, serious correction should be publicly given.

KEEP IT BIBLICAL

The following points are significant when examining progressive Christianity from a biblical worldview.

1. Truth must always be spoken in love.

> Though I speak with the tongues of men and of angels, but have not love, I have become sounding brass or a clanging cymbal (1 Corinthians 13:1).

> Let your speech always be with grace, seasoned with salt, that you may know how you ought to answer each one (Colossians 4:6).

2. Love will always adhere to and rejoice in truth.

> [Love] does not rejoice in iniquity, but rejoices in the truth (1 Corinthians 13:6).

3. The communicator of truth is not an enemy.

> "For I have not shunned to declare to you the whole counsel of God" (Acts 20:27).

> Have I therefore become your enemy because I tell you the truth? (Galatians 4:16).

4. Truth can and often does create discomfort, not for the sake of discomfort but for the sake of correction and healing.

> Faithful are the wounds of a friend,
> But the kisses of an enemy are deceitful.
> (Proverbs 27:6)

"You are already clean because of the word which I have spoken to you" (John 15:3).

For the word of God is living and powerful, and sharper than any two-edged sword, piercing even to the division of soul and spirit, and of joints and marrow, and is a discerner of the thoughts and intents of the heart (Hebrews 4:12).

5. Consensus does not determine truth, and a negative response does not indicate error.

"Enter by the narrow gate; for wide is the gate and broad is the way that leads to destruction, and there are many who go in by it. Because narrow is the gate and difficult is the way which leads to life, and there are few who find it" (Matthew 7:13-14).

KEEP IT GOING

The following are some of the questions or arguments you're likely to hear when discussing progressive Christianity, along with some suggested points for keeping the discussion going.

"Telling people they are sinful is emotionally damaging to them."

1. Overemphasizing our sin nature without emphasizing our value in God's sight is an imbalance that could be harmful. That means we should teach both, not neglect one for the other.

2. Shaming and informing are not the same. If I tell someone, "You're such an evil sinner!" I'm shaming them. If I tell someone, "All of us, you included, have fallen short of God's perfect standards. That means we've all sinned," then I'm informing and doing no harm.

3. All doctrine should be applied with wisdom, certainly, and emphasized according to need. Jesus rebuked when necessary and comforted when appropriate. We can do both.

"Warning people of hell is sadistic and seriously misrepresents the heart of God."

1. The heart of God is for people to live forever, not to die apart from Him (Ezekiel 33:11). Warning people about judgment aligns with the heart of God.

2. Overemphasizing hell at the expense of God's grace and love is wrong, but teaching what Jesus Himself said about eternity isn't sadism, it's faithful stewarding of truth.

3. No one in Scripture is more specific and graphic when referencing hell than Jesus Himself (Matthew 11:20-24; 25:41-43; Mark 9:43-44; Luke 13:24-28).

"Saying Jesus is the only way to God is exclusionary and discounts the experiences of non-Christians."

1. Where Jesus was specific, we should be too. On this issue He was very specific: "I am the way, the truth, and the life. No one comes to the Father except through Me" (John 14:6).

2. "Exclusionary" is not wrong when applied to truth. Any absolute truth by its absolute nature excludes other ideas.

3. Saying Jesus is the only way does not exclude anyone; it invites everyone by saying, "There is only one way. Please take it!"

4. This does not discount anyone's experience, but it makes a distinction between another experience and the rebirth Jesus invites us to.

"We've shown a lack of love to LGBTQ people and need to welcome them instead of judging them."

1. Many Christians have shown a lack of love to LGBTQ people and others. When that happens, we should repent.

2. Welcoming people to attend our churches is not the same as welcoming people to join our churches. Church attendance is open to anyone; church membership is open only to people who will submit their lives to the authority of Scripture.

3. Judging homosexual people outside the church is uncalled for. Judging sexual sin within the church is mandated (1 Corinthians 5:9-13).

"Gay Christians exist and should be recognized as brothers and sisters in Christ."

1. Believers who experience homosexual feelings exist, but Scripture never calls us to identify believers by or with a sinful sexual tendency.

2. Believers who embrace homosexuality exist, calling themselves gay Christians. But while we may recognize them as brothers or sisters in Christ, we must also recognize them as brothers or sisters in Christ who are in serious error.

3. We cannot be in fellowship with people who identify as Christian and who also practice unrepentant sexual sin (1 Corinthians 5:11).

"The Bible is inspiring and useful, but to place it above all other books is to denigrate the wisdom of so many others."

1. The Bible places itself above all other books with good reason (2 Timothy 3:16-17). It is God-inspired and provides

an ultimate authority to turn to for questions of doctrine and instruction.

2. Placing the Bible above other books hardly denigrates their wisdom. It only subjects the wisdom of other sources to the infallible source.

"Jesus stood with the oppressed and marginalized. So should we."

1. Jesus invited all people, both the marginalized and the powerful, to Himself.

2. Jesus stood no more with the oppressed than He did with the general population.

3. Jesus defended the oppressed and dignified the marginalized. So should we. He also, even when dignifying someone who had sinned, acknowledged they had sins to forgive (Mark 2:5) and admonished them to sin no more (John 8:11).

"Jesus rebuked the hypocrisy and self-righteousness of religious leaders. So should we."

1. No argument there. When religious leaders are hypocritical or behave like Pharisees, they should be called on it.

2. Religious leaders are not being hypocritical or behaving like Pharisees when they simply explain the nature of sin and the need for repentance.

"Young people are leaving the church because of its rigid dogma."

1. If young people leave the church because the church teaches absolutes, that is not a fault on the church's part but a rejection of those truths on the part of the young people who leave it.

2. If young people leave the church because the church lacks compassion or teaches dogma without living up to what it teaches, then the fault is with the church. The answer is to repent of the lack of compassion and the hypocrisy, not the teaching of sound doctrine.

3. We can't judge the rightness or wrongness of teaching by the way it's received. Truth was often rejected throughout Scripture; the same is true today.

"People are turned off by Christianity because they no longer see it as relevant."

1. There have always been people who rejected Christianity because they saw it as irrelevant. That doesn't make it so.

2. When Christianity is taught properly it is anything but irrelevant. It speaks to the eternal and priority issues of life.

"If you believe in a literal hell, you must be sadistic and somewhat twisted in your thinking."

1. Careful. You just called Jesus a twisted sadist.

2. To believe in hell is not the same as sadistically enjoying the idea. I hate the idea of judgment and hope to see people avoid it.

3. Overemphasizing a doctrine can be sadistic. Preaching it clearly is not.

"Jesus would never discriminate. Neither should we."

1. Jesus would not accept one person who came to Him and reject another, that is true. In that sense, He would not discriminate.

2. Jesus discriminated between right and wrong when He taught in the Gospels. He discriminates today between those who are His and those who are not, referring to His sheep as those who hear His voice (John 10:27). And He foretold a day when He would discriminate between those He knew and those He did not (Matthew 7:21-23). In that sense, Jesus did discriminate, does discriminate, and will discriminate.

3. To say there is truth versus error and right versus wrong is to discriminate. Everyone does.

"I used to believe like you, but I feel so much freer now that I embrace a more inclusive Christianity."

1. Orthodox Christianity is inclusive, welcoming everyone but not approving of everything. I doubt the form of Christianity you adhere to approves of everything. Who does?

2. I don't question whether or not you feel free, but is the feeling of freedom really the way to distinguish truth from error?

3. I am sorry if you experienced a church where love and graciousness were absent. But that doesn't mean the teachings of the church were wrong, only the way they were lived out.

"I don't want my children to grow up afraid of God or thinking they're terrible people."

1. Teaching children the Word of God makes them aware of God, not afraid of Him. Scripture reveals Him as a loving Father and Shepherd. Those are not scary images.

2. Unwisely emphasizing the wrath of God is not the same as teaching that the wrath of God exists.

3. Children are not made to think they're terrible by being

taught they're imperfect, as we all are. "Imperfect" is not the same as "without eternal value."

"Your form of Christianity is becoming less popular and progressive Christianity is gaining in popularity."

1. Truth is never unproven by its unpopularity.

2. Error is never made true by its popularity.

3. Majority opinion works for a democracy, but not as a way of determining absolute, eternal truths.

> *"Our forefathers were particular about maintaining landmarks; they had strong notions about fixed points of revealed doctrine, and were very tenacious of what they believed to be scriptural; their fields were protected by hedges and ditches, but their sons have grubbed up the hedges, filled up the ditches, laid all level, and played at leap-frog with the boundary stones."*
>
> CHARLES SPURGEON

CHAPTER ELEVEN

ONE LAST STAND

W e must always take sides," Nobel laureate Elie Wiesel said. "Neutrality helps the oppressor, never the victim. Silence encourages the tormenter, never the tormented."[1]

We're not asking for a fight. On the contrary, most of the tensions in America between the church and culture come from the culture trying to tell the church what to say or do, not vice versa. However strongly we may feel about issues, we're not the ones going on social media trying to silence people, or on Amazon trying to ban books, or on college campuses shouting down speakers we disagree with. We've sought to converse, not coerce, so taking sides is something many of us have been reluctant to do.

When you take sides you define, and when you define, you can alienate. So in some situations, you'll choose not to alienate by not taking a stand. There can be wisdom in that.

Unless the issue is vital, conscience is at stake, and you find yourself remembering that if you're ashamed of His words, He'll someday be ashamed of you (Luke 9:26). That's when Wiesel's advice on taking a side resonates.

My wife and I found ourselves in that position in the mid-1980s. We were engaged, and by then I'd been away from the gay community for a few years. But I still had gay friends who understood my decision and beliefs, and though they disagreed, we were on good terms. A couple of them had even met Renee, and we'd all gotten along well, so they invited us to attend a birthday party at their home.

We went with no agenda other than to wish one of them a happy birthday and to enjoy a summer afternoon with them and their friends by the pool. It was a large gathering, almost exclusively gay, and for the first hour or so we mingled, munched on snacks, and enjoyed a lot of small talk.

Then one of the guests, an attorney who'd had one too many wine coolers and felt like arguing, cornered me on the patio and loudly asked, "Why are you two here?"

Funny how quiet a patio full of partygoers can suddenly get. Even the disco music seemed to whisper.

"We're friends of Rich and Bud's and wanted to wish Bud a happy birthday," I said, aware that every word I said from then on would be scrutinized.

"Well, how do you know them?" he asked.

"Oh, I met them a few years ago." I shrugged, hoping he'd go for ambiguity.

Fat chance. "Well, are you gay or what?"

The Mental Committee shot me a quick memo: *Be clear, not coy!*

Renee sat down beside me while I explained that I had met our hosts before I had decided, as a Christian, that gay relationships weren't an option for me anymore.

Another drunken guest shouted out, "Oh, I was raised Baptist, and all you people are [expletive deleted]." Yet another said, "I'm Mormon, but I guess I'm not doing it right," which we laughingly agreed with. Then the attorney said, "Hey, everybody, let's all say what we think about God and religion. I'd really like to hear this."

Some gay pool party this is turning out to be! I thought. But amazingly, one guest after another offered their views on spirituality very freely and, I must say, very respectfully. Then it was Renee's turn, so she gave her testimony about hearing the gospel, being saved, navigating some rough times in life, and learning to lean on the Lord.

"Sounds like you're both Jerry Falwell's people," someone said, while a couple of the women playfully threatened to throw Renee in the pool. She grinned like a good sport, then it was my turn.

"You know, Jerry Falwell had nothing to do with my decision," I said. "I had to look at what the Scriptures say about life and family, and I knew I had to choose. So I chose, and I found peace. And isn't choice something we all value? I never chose to be attracted to men, for sure, but I did choose what to do with my attractions. You know what? I'm glad I did."

Taking sides was called for. In doing so, we alienated some, amused others, and won a few over to a better understanding of the faith. We hadn't come to take positions, but when put on the spot, we had to.

WHILE IT'S STILL LIGHT

The window of opportunity to openly speak truth is closing. That doesn't mean we'll stop speaking it, but we'll soon meet barriers and dangers that aren't in place now. So now's the time to, as Jesus said, "work the works of Him who sent Me [and us] while it is day; the night is coming when no one can work" (John 9:4).

If there's a right position to take, we have limited time to take it freely because a lot has changed in the thirty-plus years since that reasonably friendly pool party. The movement to stop all communication of "unacceptable views" is now worldwide and popular, a modern Goliath bellowing threats and daring anyone to challenge him.

Too many of us won't, for reasons that are understandable but not legitimate.

Some of us don't like the way Christians in the past have addressed these issues. We remember prominent pastors or televangelists making outrageous remarks about gays or feminists or liberals, and we're determined never to sound like them or be linked to them.

I call that the Archie Bunker syndrome. In the seventies sitcom *All in the Family*, the main character named Archie Bunker was a social conservative who was insensitive, bigoted, verbally clumsy, ill-informed, and full of himself. He was the perfect buffoon for anyone wanting to think the worst of conservatives, and an embarrassment to conservatives as well. So much so, in fact, that many conservatives became reluctant to identify themselves. They weren't ashamed of their values, but they were mighty ashamed of the Archie Bunker image and wanted no attachment to it.

There are believers today feeling a similar embarrassment over the image of the so-called Religious Right. Because some well-known Christians spoke irresponsibly in the past, and because their remarks get endlessly rehashed to discredit the rest of us, some take the bait and refuse to speak. They won't take sides because of the way others did.

But Jesus took clear sides on monotheism (Mark 12:29), the value of the Law (Matthew 5:17-19), the sin of adultery (Matthew 19:9), and the call to holiness (Matthew 5:48). Those were sides the Pharisees had already taken, in all the wrong ways and with the worst attitudes. Yet Jesus didn't shy away from declaring a truth just because someone else had declared it the wrong way. On the contrary, He took His positions all the more plainly, with love, authority, and clarity. He knew they were vital; He knew they were relevant. Even if they had been presented poorly in the past.

Others won't take sides because they don't want to alienate. With the best of intentions, they'll say, "Hey, I don't want my positions to turn people away, I just want to share Jesus."

But nobody ever wanted to share Jesus more than Jesus Himself did. After all, He's the one who said He'd come to seek and to save the lost (Luke 19:10), who invited everyone to come to Him (Matthew 11:28), and who still invites everyone to come to Him (Revelation 22:17).

That never kept Him from taking positions. When He defined marriage in unalterable terms (Matthew 19:4-9), He knew some wouldn't care for it and even said so (Matthew 19:11). Ditto for when He described hell (Mark 9:43-48), condemned lust (Matthew 5:28), and exposed hypocrisy (Matthew 23:13-36). The love He felt for a rich young man didn't keep Him from saying something He knew would alienate the man (Matthew 19:16-22), and the love He felt for all people didn't keep Him from warning them of the cross they would carry and the life they would die to if they followed Him (Luke 9:23-24).

Clearly, He wanted people to come to Him. Equally clear was His refusal to compromise for the sake of converts.

If we're not upfront with people about vital issues, then we become dishonest, evasive, and ill-equipped to get anyone thinking about truth. We also misrepresent God by telling people what we think they want to hear, worrying more about the response to our message and less about its clarity.

That's a problem. Paul referred to himself and his co-workers as "ambassadors for Christ" (2 Corinthians 5:20). An ambassador has a twofold job description: first, to faithfully represent the principles and message of the one who sent him. Second, as much as possible, he wants to build goodwill in the process. Both are important, but the first trumps the second. Imagine that ambassador reporting home and saying, "I didn't deliver your message, sir, because I didn't think they'd like it. But hey, I sure did get the people to like me, so mission accomplished!"

Likewise, when we say we want to "win" people, we've got to ask ourselves what we want to win them to. If we simply get them to like us or feel more comfortable with us, that's well and good. But if in our desire to be liked, we leave them without the clear direction truth provides, then we've also left them without the guidance and tools that come with the full counsel of God. If they refuse to accept that guidance and those tools, that's on them. But if we refuse to give that guidance and those tools, that's on us.

Jesus didn't refuse to give them, yet the way He handled truth made it all the easier for those who would receive it. First, He prioritized. When talking to a Samaritan woman in sexual sin, He prioritized the message of who He was and what He offered (John 4:10) over the topic of her sin, which He acknowledged without overemphasizing (John 4:17-18). He kept the main thing the main thing.

Second, He leveled the playing field. He publicly condemned lust (Matthew 5:28), religiosity (Matthew 6:1-8), fornication (Matthew 15:17-20), selfishness (Matthew 5:41-42), adultery (John 8:11), and unforgiveness (Matthew 6: 14-15) with equal emphasis. He was not known just for being anti-sexual sin or anti-cruelty. No one could say of Him (as people often say of us) that He was a Johnny-one-note,

thundering against the juicy sins while winking at the more acceptable ones.

Third, He could relate though He disapproved. The fact He was
able to eat with tax collectors (Luke 5:29) and interact with prostitutes
(Luke 7:36-38) is telling. He disapproved of their sins, yet His disapproval didn't prevent Him from enjoying a relationship with them.

For example, He was against greed, but I doubt He told the tax col-
lector He was dining with, "Pass the bread, if you're not too greedy."
He was against fornication, but I don't see Him telling the harlot who
bathed His feet with her hair, "Be sure to get the toes, hussy!" I've no
doubt He engaged with sinners, relating to them in a friendly human-
to-human way, loving them, listening to them, speaking general truths
about God, and specific truths about sin. He was, as John said, "full of
grace and truth." His ability to relate wasn't approval, and His disapproval wasn't an inability to relate.

We ought, John said, to walk as He did (1 John 2:6). Among other
things, that means we should handle truth as He did, which we can. We
can relate respectfully to all people, answer honest questions when they
arise, initiate conversations about current issues as wisdom and opportunity allow, maintain clear positions in our homes and churches, express
those positions in the public arena, and keep our priorities straight.

We'll get pushback when we do, even threats. Worse yet, we're
already seeing the state and the Cancel Culture merge in their efforts to
reach into our homes and churches, telling us what we may say, teach,
and practice. This should be alarming to anyone who cares about truth.

But if we say we're alarmed about people trying to silence the truth,
that implies we hold the truth in high regard. If so, then we've got some
hard questions to ask about our own approach toward it.

Truth's survival, thank God, doesn't depend on us. It keeps breath-
ing whether or not it's acknowledged, so our faithfulness to it doesn't
make it or break it. Our faithfulness to it does something else, though.
It largely determines whether some people will live or die, and whether
we who are alive in Christ will be fervent or lukewarm. The practical
value we place on the doctrines we say we believe will determine an outcome for us and for countless others.

When Goliath challenged Israel, no one seemed fit to respond until a lad with faith, boldness, and the right weapons stepped up. It's not a stretch to say that today we're on the verge of stepping up or stepping down in the face of a giant's threat. Nothing less than our own faith, without which it's impossible to please God (Hebrews 11:6), our own boldness, a quality defining the early church (Acts 4:31), and the right weapons, which are mighty though not natural (2 Corinthians 10:4-6) will be required.

So as truth becomes more widely and violently opposed, will we make a fresh commitment, personally and collectively, to learn it and to live it?

Much of the dysfunction we see in modern Christianity, a dysfunction making us less than fit for battle, stems from neglect of one of those two—ignorance of the truth or ignoring the truth.

Too many of us are not learning the truth very well because biblical ignorance among Christians is a modern scandal.[2] We're also not living it well because moral failure and personal irresponsibility among believers are even greater scandals. We're not expressing it that well, either, because too few of us are speaking, while too many of us are either saying the wrong things or saying the right things in the wrong way.

If our goal is faithful stewardship of truth, then we've got our work cut out for us. We may be able to refute the accusations Cancel Culture makes about us, but using the truth to combat a lie is simpler, and probably easier, then applying it to ourselves. As the philosopher Alfred Adler famously said, "It is always easier to fight for one's principles than to live up to them."[3]

If we're going to live up to our principles, we've got to know and understand them. On this point, letters from Paul, John, Peter, and James remind us of the early Christians' approach to truth. Read their epistles, along with Luke's account of the church's birth and expansion in the book of Acts, and you see a lovely simplicity.

To them, people were either saved or unsaved, alive in Christ or dead in sin. Doctrines were true or false; behaviors moral or immoral; believers spiritually mature or carnally stunted. Truth was vital, a hill to readily die on, demanding private obedience, regular reinforcement, and the unintimidated proclamation of heralds trumpeting a life or death message.

"Let a man so consider us," Paul said, "as servants of Christ and stewards of the mysteries of God. Moreover, it is required in stewards that one be found faithful" (1 Corinthians 4:1-2). If we're accounted as stewards of truth, God grant we be found faithful in our stewardship. That way we can better address the errors around us while staying immune to their influence.

LEARNING THE TRUTH

New Testament scholar David Nienhuis had some discouraging words to say when commenting on how well, or how poorly, evangelicals know their Bible:

> For well over twenty years now, Christian leaders have been lamenting the loss of general biblical literacy in America...Some among us may be tempted to seek odd solace in the recognition that our culture is increasingly post-Christian...Much to our embarrassment, however, it has become increasingly clear that the situation is really no better among confessing Christians, even those who claim to hold the Bible in high regard.[4]

If those holding the Bible in high regard neglect it, they're hardly in a position to express it, much less defend it. We don't expect adult functioning from children.

There's the problem. Christians who don't know the Word aren't just unlearned, they're immature. The author of Hebrews pointed this out when he lamented:

> For though by this time you ought to be teachers, you need someone to teach you again the first principles of the oracles of God; and you have come to need milk and not solid food. For everyone who partakes only of milk is unskilled

in the word of righteousness, for he is a babe. But solid food belongs to those who are of full age, that is, those who by reason of use have their senses exercised to discern both good and evil (Hebrews 5:12-14).

He's not addressing new believers here, since he plainly says they should be further along by now. They've been believers for some time, but it doesn't show in their knowledge of the most basic doctrines, nor in their spiritual maturity, since ignorance of basic truth leaves them unequipped to discern good and evil.

By ignoring a routine study of the Word, Christians can't know much about the God they believe in nor the life they're meant to be living. When Christians don't know, they don't grow.

Two things have to come as a result, the first being general instability. Isaac made a bleak prediction about his son Reuben when he prophesied, "Unstable as water, you shall not excel" (Genesis 49:4). Instability is a symptom of immaturity, showing itself in impulsiveness, impatience, self-centeredness, and all the other traits we associate with childishness.

So is it any surprise when Christians who neglect the Word don't attain spiritual adulthood? How else can we account for the number of believers who church hop, leaving one church after another over minor irritations or boredom? Or for the high level of porn use and sexual impurity in our ranks, the susceptibility to false teachings, or the ease with which too many of us are offended, terminating relationships, and then jumping into new ones?

That spells instability, a predictable symptom of immaturity, which is a predictable symptom of biblical ignorance. But another symptom of biblical ignorance emerges as well, which is a lack of biblical discernment.

When you have a working knowledge of a document, attained by reading and studying it regularly, then you can discern whether something is in agreement with or opposition to that document.

I've read Dickens's *A Tale of Two Cities* countless times, well into the double digits. No other novel keeps moving me as this one does, so I read it through at least every couple of years. Because I've read it thoroughly, I also have a good working knowledge of it.

That's why I can tell you what it says or doesn't say, and with that knowledge I can tell you if something is harmonious to the book or contradictory.

I know, for example, that Lucie Manette deeply loved Charles Darnay and was also fond of Sydney Carton as a friend, though he in turn was mad about her. So if you tell me that Lucy was romantically torn between two men, or that Carton loathed her, I'll know that's wrong because I've read and reread Dickens's description of the relationship between the three. If you tell me the Vengeance babysat for children of aristocrats, I'll know that's wrong too because I know how the Vengeance felt about the aristocracy. I know the book, so when I hear someone say something that's not in it, or take something out of context, I can discern that.

Without that discernment I might fall for someone's misinterpretation of Dickens's classic. No tragedy there, but it's tragic indeed when Christians fall for distortions of the Bible because they lack the biblical discernment biblical study produces. I've seen more than one believer fall for the pro-gay theology, or the critical race theory, or the Universalist approach to salvation, or humanism, feminism, Gnosticism, or legalism, all because their ignorance of the Book left them open to its misrepresentation.

If the church cannot discern truth from error, then we'll lack a foundation from which to preach to the lost or to build up the redeemed. Needless to say, we'll also be unable to speak from a biblical worldview to the errors in our culture. In fact, we'll most likely absorb those errors into our own thinking.

"Tell me what the world is saying today," the late Francis Schaeffer wrote, "and I'll tell you what the church will be saying in seven years."[5] Considering what the world is saying today, God grant that Schaeffer turns out to be wrong. If he's not, then apologist Greg Bahnsen's warning may well apply: "When the church begins to look and sound like the world there is no compelling rationale for its continued existence."[6]

Fortunately, after chiding the Hebrews for their spiritual immaturity and encouraging them to grow in doctrinal knowledge, the author concludes: "And this we will do if God permits" (Hebrews 6:3).

So will we, and there are simple ways we can.

We can make and keep a commitment to daily study the Word, at least one chapter per day, as a way of life.

These times call for strong, well-grounded believers. They remind us that in the body of Christ, our need for the mutual upbuilding we give each other in fellowship is keen. But that, in turn, means each of us needs to be healthy and functioning, else how can we build each other up? Your spiritual vitality (or lack thereof) impacts the rest of us, just as the health (or lack thereof) of a body part impacts the rest of the body. So it's not just you who needs to be nourished by the Word. We your teammates need you to be nourished by it too, because we need you strong, and no woman or man ever got strong in Christ without also getting strong in the Word.

We can also support and encourage the teachers we listen to who faithfully minister the Word.

This is an age of progressive Christians, false teachers, extremists, and court jesters influencing thousands. They have their followings and celebrity status, much to the heartache of the many responsible stewards of the Bible who plug along, teaching from the pulpit, podcast, or Christian radio. They need to hear that you appreciate their voice of truth in a time of error, and they need to be reminded that, as Paul reminded the Corinthians, their "labor is not in vain in the Lord" (1 Corinthians 15:58). So be sure you're giving verbal, prayerful, and financial support to your local church and to the ministries that regularly benefit you. It's simply wrong to take what they offer and give nothing in return.

We can also be more careful to measure the legitimacy of any ministry, whether a megachurch, a parachurch group, a television ministry, or a local congregation, not by its leader's charm or eloquence or good looks or dynamic methods, but by his fidelity to the Word of God, both in his teaching and in his way of life.

Biblical discernment, acquired by biblical knowledge, calls us to ask more of our leaders than the ability to sway a crowd. Today, thank

God, we have excellent teachers of the Word who build up the church daily with expository teaching and commentary. But too often others are raised up solely on their giftings. They bring to the table a dramatic testimony, physical beauty, and stellar communication skills, qualities that provide a somewhat inspiring entertainment, which is enough milk to charm a flock but not enough meat to feed it.

Worse, when someone charming teaches error, the error is easier to digest, and loyalty to a pleasing personality can cause his followers to defend him because he's likeable, though lacking. So before saying "Amen" to anyone out of politeness, let's revive a more Berean approach to assessing ministry (Acts 17:11). If Paul himself was subject to that kind of scrutiny, surely today's Christian leaders shouldn't balk at it.

Learning and becoming grounded in truth is a first crucial step when responding to the times. One of the most important questions anyone can ask was asked by Saul of Tarsus upon his conversion: "Lord, what do You want me to do?" (Acts 9:6).

Let's consider Paul's words to the Romans for a response: "What does the Scripture say?" (Romans 4:3).

LIVING THE TRUTH

What's been learned should be lived; what's not lived may as well not have been learned. So said James:

> But be doers of the word, and not hearers only, deceiving yourselves. For if anyone is a hearer of the word and not a doer, he is like a man observing his natural face in a mirror; for he observes himself, goes away, and immediately forgets what kind of man he was. But he who looks into the perfect law of liberty and continues in it, and is not a forgetful hearer but a doer of the work, this one will be blessed in what he does (James 1:22-25).

My mirror tells me things, some good, some not. If it tells me I'm overweight, I need to act on that information. If it tells me my clothes match, then I need to wear them. If it tells me I'm pale, I need to consult a doctor. If it tells me I'm disheveled, then I need to spruce up. If I don't act on the info I get from the mirror, then looking at it didn't accomplish much.

Having the right positions is good. Living them is better and a necessary foundation for rising to Goliath's challenge.

Which raises the need for higher credibility. In his letter to the Romans, Paul asked a rhetorical question:

> You, therefore, who teach another, do you not teach yourself? You who preach that a man should not steal, do you steal? You who say, "Do not commit adultery," do you commit adultery? You who abhor idols, do you rob temples? You who make your boast in the law, do you dishonor God through breaking the law? (Romans 2:21-23).

Condemning the hypocrisy of people who don't follow what they preach, he also points out the effect of hypocrisy on credibility: "For the name of God is blasphemed among the Gentiles because of you" (Romans 2:24).

One of the commonest reasons people give for rejecting Christianity is hypocrisy among believers, a willingness to publicly declare what we privately ignore. They say we present a strange, disjointed portrait: people who condemn gay marriage but hop in and out of marriages; people who condemn dishonesty but privately defraud in business; people who condemn sleazy television but privately view porn; people who condemn fornication but often sleep together before marriage.

We can debate how accurate this portrait is, and we should. But we can't call it completely inaccurate either. While most Christians aren't guilty of gross hypocrisy, the percentage who are (both among leadership and laity) is way too high, and the world knows it.

Samson's strength came not just from muscularity but from separation. So long as he adhered to his vow of separation to God, including the vow not to cut his hair, he retained his strength. When he compromised that vow by allowing his hair to be cut, his power was gone (Judges 16).

In today's church the number of people refusing to live separated lives—whether through use of porn, dependency on alcohol or drugs, sex before marriage, sex outside of marriage, indifference to the poor, carelessness in relationships, or carelessness in speech—constitutes a haircut we can't afford. Where there's compromised holiness, there will always be compromised power and compromised credibility. Deficient in those two areas, we'll never be fit for today's challenges.

But fitness isn't just attained by trying harder. It's also attained through honesty and allies. If someone is serious about getting in shape, he'll first honestly assess the problem by looking at the scale, then develop allies to coach him, train with him, and cheer him on.

Holiness, likewise, isn't a solo act. Thousands of Christians have developed private patterns and indulgences that aren't easily broken and are certain to stay locked in place without being brought to the light. That means confession and accountability, two elements we've got to get more serious about if we want to attain, then maintain, moral integrity and the strength that comes with it.

Many of us need to confess our private sins to a person, not just to God. The refusal to bring them to the light before others is the stronghold keeping the porn, the affair, the gluttony, the whatever alive. So James said, "Confess your trespasses to one another, and pray for one another, that you may be healed" (James 5:16). The author of Hebrews added, "Exhort one another daily, while it is called 'Today,' lest any of you be hardened through the deceitfulness of sin" (Hebrews 3:13).

Here is where many us need to stop kidding ourselves. The longer we keep secret sins in the dark, the easier it becomes to be "hardened through the deceitfulness of sin" and believe they're not a big deal. We'll quit someday soon. We're entitled.

Until we get more real with each other, we won't get much further in power and credibility. Unconfessed, our sins will stay intact and overcome us. Unaccountable, we'll nurture those sins until they get too big to be hidden and we become one more statistic in the roster of

Christian failures. If we claim to love truth, then surely we'll be willing to abandon our lies.

IN REFORM AND REVIVAL

What we're facing, then, is nothing short of a need for reform in the hope of revival. The church fit to respond with grace and truth to the Cancel Culture will be one that's reformed by a return to basics and revived by a fresh wind.

In that church, members will know their primary responsibility is to love God. They'll also know they cannot love a God they do not know, and they'll realize God is best known through prayer and the study of His Word. So they'll invest daily in their intimacy with Him through prayer and study, growing in love for Him as a result, and growing in the obedience born of love. Jesus said, "If you love Me, keep My commandments" (John 14:15). To know Him is to love Him, and to study His Word and pray daily is the best way to know Him. With knowledge comes love; with love comes obedience. That simplicity of daily devotion will be business as usual among believers.

Members of that church will take their relationships with each other seriously, continuing regularly in fellowship, group prayer, mutual study, and breaking of bread together, as did the early church (Acts 2:42-47). They will be involved in each other's lives, tending to each other's physical, material, spiritual, and emotional needs. Because of that, their church will be to them a necessity, not an optional luxury. Their participation in its life will be vital, a covenant between them and their leaders and fellow parishioners to give of themselves and stay rooted and grounded in the congregation, leaving only for the most serious or unavoidable of reasons.

Members of that church will hold a biblical worldview, judging truth versus error and right versus wrong by Scripture. Studying the Word privately and collectively, they'll have the discernment needed to make those judgments. They'll teach sound doctrine to all ages, and they won't shy away from talking about hot-button issues to their youth, because they'll know the culture wants to make its case to their children, so they'll want to make their case first. That's why they'll talk openly, from a biblical perspective, about all issues raised in this book and other issues prominent in their time and place.

Members of that church won't leave evangelism to full-time evangelists. They'll share their testimonies whenever and wherever they can, wisely and respectfully. They'll bring unsaved friends and loved ones to church, encouraging them to continue coming and praying regularly for their hearts to be reached. They'll disciple new believers and strengthen mature ones, because they'll recognize and exercise the benefits of body ministry (Romans 12:4-8).

That's the reformed church kneeling together in an upper room, waiting on God, and receiving a fresh wind to revive them and send them out in power. That's the church with a state-of-the-art sling to face the giant's threat, a body of believers knowing and living the truth, and thereby fit to teach it, express it, defend it.

THE ANCIENT PAIN

That's also a church facing hard times, with hard decisions to make. The truths we hold are becoming lightning rods to an increasingly hostile environment.

If current trends continue, churches, Christian universities, and nonprofit religious organizations will face revocation of their tax-exempt status or of their state funding for student loans if they don't change their policies on gender identity and sexual behavior. They'll also face lawsuits from students, former members, or visitors who claim to have been harmed by the messages or practices the church adheres to.

Corporations may force their Christian employees to choose between attending training events that conflict with their conscience or losing their jobs. Students may find themselves disciplined or expelled for holding positions that are unacceptable to their schools. Parents may be classified as "abusive" for not confirming their children's orientation or gender identity and might suffer their forcible removal from their homes.

Pastors, counselors, teachers, or leaders of any sort may be subject to a fine or jail time if they speak biblically on homosexuality or trans-genderism. Churches, in fact, may eventually be subject to state licens-ing to determine their qualifications to hold services and their leader's compliance with the government's standards of doctrine.

If Christ tarries, there will soon be a high price to pay for sound doctrine. Collectively, we'll need to strategize, inform, and equip each other, while continuing to pray we avoid raving or caving in the face of oppression.

Individually, some of us are already paying that price. We've been rejected by those we love the most, labeled "toxic" or "hateful," dis-carded as infidels unworthy of love or friendship. It's not just the pain of having a prodigal. It's the pain of becoming, without your consent, your prodigal's enemy.

You didn't attend his wedding. You don't agree with her racial pol-itics. You won't call him by a female name. You can't affirm there are multiple ways to God. You vote, speak, and live your conscience. All of these have been deemed unforgiveable, and you're the unforgiven.

This is the ancient pain of resistance and rejection, experienced when resistance was the only option and rejection the outcome.

From the beginning, God's people have faced individuals, trends, or government powers demanding things they simply couldn't com-ply with, so they resisted. They also learned, as do we, that holding to truth can put you in a very lonely place.

That's when the pain of rejection sets in, a kick in the gut deliv-ered from parties we never expected a kick from: our government, our friends, our family. The nation we love rejects the God who blessed it from formation to the present, and we grieve. Friends we thought we knew switch positions on key issues and suddenly decide they need to convert us or harass us for not converting. Family members who know better accuse us of harming them by simply continuing to be who we've always been.

There's no way to blithely sail through this. We can know we're in the right, but that doesn't eliminate the hurt we feel over the rejec-tion or the anger we feel over the injustice. Remember, Jesus Himself wept over Jerusalem, knowing full well He was right, but longing over them all the same (Luke 19:41-44). Fidelity to truth brings peace, but it won't eliminate pain.

In earlier chapters we've looked at some guidelines for the conversations we're likely to have. But what about the pain we're likely to feel?

It's inevitable. To love is to be held hostage by the objects of your love, for better or worse. If they live within the truth, your heart will be full and you'll agree with John that "I have no greater joy than to hear that my children walk in truth" (3 John 4). If not, your heart will ache over their present state and fear for their future one. It's tempting to try resolving that pain by revising truth or killing love. If you revise the truth, you can quit worrying about your loved one being outside it. If you kill love, you get the same result—no love, no worries.

Obviously neither is a legitimate option. If you know the truth and you love people, then you'll feel pain when the people you love reject the truth you know and you along with it.

But it's also instructive. One of our highest goals as followers of Jesus is to, as Paul said, "know Him and the power of His resurrection, and the fellowship of His sufferings" (Philippians 3:10).

Funny how those three seem to come in order. I came to know Him as a teenager, and I can feel the day it happened as though it was happening now. The joy was, as the hymn says, "unspeakable and full of glory," and my newfound walk with Him was marked by daily elation.

The power of His resurrection came next. I experienced it through deliverance from sin, power to witness and preach, and even (on one memorable occasion) the power to pray for the sick and see results! The power of His resurrection was manifest in so many ways during my young adulthood.

But the fellowship of His sufferings? It would be decades before I had a clue what they were. Only then, when I began to love with depth, could I be introduced to that sacred fellowship. Then I learned, and am still learning, to weep in hope over a country decaying from within, and over backslidden friends, hurting loved ones, and (if you can bear the melodrama of it) the misery of the human condition. Pain is a lesson book teaching me what His heart is like, how far mine still is from His, and how I need to lean on Him when the emotions get rough because just as He said, apart from Him I can do nothing (John 15:5).

But finally, while being inevitable and instructive, the pain is also indicative of God's intentions. When He heard Israel's cry, He intervened. When Jesus was moved with compassion, He acted. Pain is an indicator that something is wrong which God seeks to make right. In that sense, pain carries strong elements of hope.

When we hurt over someone's error, we enter into agreement with God that the error is wrong. We speak to the person as we are able, then we intercede, believing that if our hearts ache over a loved one, how much more does God's? And if God was moved with compassion in the past, He surely is moved in the now.

There is our hope. Our pain is a reminder of what God continues to feel and will act on. No wonder, then, the psalmist hopefully declares, "Those who sow in tears shall reap in joy" (Psalm 126:5). Even creation itself, according to Paul, is in pain, groaning over its own condition, waiting for the final restoration (Romans 8:18-22). Pain not only says something is wrong. It also says something can be made right.

For now, things are far from right. Truth is increasingly despised along with its messengers. But oddly enough, the vilification of truth is also its verification. Paul confirmed this in his letter to the Philippians: "and not in any way terrified by your adversaries, which is to them a proof of perdition, but to you of salvation" (Philippians 1:28).

Each vehement opposition is an affirmation of truth, and an indictment against its opponents. But if truth has the power to agitate, it also has the power to regenerate. It remains something "living and powerful, and sharper than any two-edged sword" (Hebrews 4:12), that won't return void (Isaiah 55:11), and a treasure entrusted to us (1 Corinthians 4:1). We have solid reason to trust its power to save, to liberate, and to still change the course of history, if God wills.

I'll admit to closing this book with sadness over these strange, dark times. In that sense, I appreciate John the Baptist's forlorn communication to Jesus when he was unjustly imprisoned, and what had seemed so promising was now looking so bleak. He wrote like a man in despair when he asked: "Are you the Coming One, or do we look for another?" (Matthew 11:3).

Jesus gently admonished him in response: "The blind see and the lame walk; the lepers are cleansed and the deaf hear; the dead are raised up and the poor have the gospel preached to them" (Matthew 11:5).

Recognizing John's discouragement, the Lord essentially said, "Your temporary hardship doesn't spell defeat for My eternal purposes. They will continue. You play your part, and you'll reap your reward. But the unshakeable kingdom will come and cannot be stopped."

There it is. God is not mocked, we are still more than conquerors, and the truth cannot be cancelled by even the most aggressive culture. We can weep, but still sing, then, alongside the millions of saints who for ages have rejoiced in how firm our foundation still is and how solid the rock we still stand on.

Our hope continues to be built on nothing less, because as long as the people of God are ready to speak the Word of God, and as long as the Spirit of God is ready to confirm the Word of God, then the people of God need never fear that the Word of God will be silenced.

Some of us may be.

But it, and He, will not.

"Do not be overcome by evil, but overcome evil with good."

Romans 12:21

NOTES

CHAPTER TWO: OF RAVERS AND CAVERS

1. Douglas Quan, "Legal Dispute Between Trans Child and Father Takes New Turn Over Freedom of Expression," *National Post*, April 30, 2019, https://nationalpost.com/news/canada/legal-dispute-between-trans-child-and-father-takes-new-turn-over-freedom-of-expression.

2. "State Rep @BrianSimsPA says he'll pay his followers $100 if they are able to dox three teen girls he films who are quietly praying outside a Planned Parenthood abortion clinic. How is this guy still allowed to be on Twitter?," https://twitter.com/LilaGraceRose/status/1125517225757007872?ref_src=twsrc%5Etfw%7Ctwcamp%5Etweetembed%7Ctwterm%5E1125749760575647744&ref_url=https%3A%2F%2Fwww.usatoday.com%2Fstory%2Fnews%2Fpolitics%2Fonpolitics%2F2019%2F05%2F07%2Fbrian-sims-pa-democratic-lawmaker-harasses-anti-abortion-activists%2F1127958001%2F.

3. Evan Sernoffsky, "Video Shows Man Kicking 85-Year-Old Antiabortion Demonstrator Outside Planned Parenthood in San Francisco," *San Francisco Chronicle*, March 27, 2019, www.sfchronicle.com/crime/article/Video-shows-man-kicking-85-year-old-antiabortion-13721975.php.

4. "Ellen DeGeneres Defends Friendship with George W. Bush," *CNN Entertainment*, October 8, 2019, www.cnn.com/videos/entertainment/2019/10/08/ellen-degeneres-george-w-bush-at-nfl-game-orig-vstop-bdk.cnn.

5. "Hillsong Pastor, Carl Lentz, Compromises on Murdering Children," www.youtube.com/watch?v=JIaUmGiuGQ4.

6. Steve Warren, "'Shameful and Demonic': Hillsong NYC Pastor Speaks Out Against New NY Abortion Law," *CBN News*, January 29, 2019, www1.cbn.com/cbnnews/us/2019/january/shameful-and-demonic-hillsong-nyc-pastor-speaks-out-against-new-ny-abortion-law.

7. Steve Warren, "Christian Singer Lauren Daigle on Homosexuality: 'I Can't Say One Way or the Other. I'm Not God,'" *CBN News*, December 3, 2018, www1.cbn.com/cbnnews/2018/december/christian-singer-lauren-daigle-on-homosexuality-i-cant-say-one-way-or-the-other-im-not-god.

8. Benjamin Sledge, "Let's Stop Pretending Christianity Is Even 'Christian' Anymore," *Heartsupport*, October 8, 2018, https://blog.heartsupport.com/lets-stop-pretending-christianity-is-even-christian-anymore-455f8897ba74.

9. Martin Luther Quotes, *GoodReads*, www.goodreads.com/quotes/657155-if-i-profess-with-the-loudest-voice-and-clearest-exposition.

CHAPTER THREE: YOU'VE BEEN SERVED

1. "Cancel Culture," *Dictionary.com*, www.dictionary.com/e/pop-culture/cancel-culture.

2. "What It Means to Get 'Canceled,'" *Merriam-Webster Dictionary*, 2020, www.merriam-webster.com/words-at-play/cancel-culture-words-were-watching.

3. "Mob Riots Aren't About George Floyd; They're About Cancel Culture, Says Horace" National Policy Center for Public Research, July 27, 2020, https://nationalcenter.org/ncppr/2020/07/27/mob-riots-arent-about-george-floyd-theyre-about-cancel-culture-says-horace-cooper/.

4. "Cancel Culture," *Cambridge Dictionary,* Cambridge University Press, 2020, https://dictionary .cambridge.org/us/dictionary/english/cancel-culture.

5. Ibid.

6. Julia Reinstein, "This Restaurant Kicked Out Sarah Sanders and a Lot of People Are Yelling About It," *Buzz Feed News,* June 23, 2018, www.buzzfeednews.com/article/juliareinstein/ sarah-sanders-kicked-out-restaurant.

7. Jamie Ehrlich, "Maxine Waters Encourages Supporters to Harass Trump Administration Officials," *CNN,* June 25, 2018, www.cnn.com/2018/06/25/politics/maxine-waters-trump-officials/ index.html.

8. "Videos of Pennsylvania Lawmaker Berating Pro-Life Demonstrators Spark Outrage and Calls for Criminal Investigation," *Channel 10 Philadelphia,* May 10, 2019, www.nbcphiladelphia.com/ news/local/pennsylvania-brian-sims-video-pro-life-demonstrators-planned-parenthood/199591/.

9. Ibid.

10. John Hinderaker, "Keith Ellison Endorses Political Violence," *Center for the American Experiment,* January, www.americanexperiment.org/2018/01/keith-ellison-endorses-political-violence/.

11. Benjy Sarlin, "O'Rourke Says Churches Against Gay Marriage Should Lose Tax Benefits, Draws Backlash," *NBC News,* October 11, 2019, www.nbcnews.com/politics/2020-election/o-rourke-says -churches-against-gay-marriage-should-lose-tax-n1065186.

12. Jeffrey J. Selingo, "College Students Support Free Speech—Unless It Offends Them," *Washington Post,* March 11, 2018, www.washingtonpost.com/local/college-students-support-free-speech -unless-it-offends-them/2018/03/09/79f21c9e-23e4-11e8-94da-ebf9d112159c_story.html.

13. Steve Warren, "Christian Singer Lauren Daigle on Homosexuality: 'I Can't Say One Way or The Other. I'm Not God,'" *CBN News,* December 3, 2018, www1.cbn.com/cbnnews/2018/december/ christian-singer-lauren-daigle-on-homosexuality-i-cant-say-one-way-or-the-other-im-not-god.

14. Chuck Schilkenstaff, "Manny Pacquiao Stands By His Views Against Homosexuality: 'You Know What I Am Telling Is the Truth,'" *Los Angeles Times,* February 19, 2016, www.latimes.com/sports/ sportsnow/la-sp-sn-manny-pacquiao-happy-god-20160219-story.html.

15. Kelly McBride, "Did George Floyd Die or Was He Murdered? One of Many Ethics Questions NPR Must Answer," *NPR,* June 4, 2020, www.npr.org/sections/publiceditor/2020/06/04/868969745/ did-george-floyd-die-or-was-he-murdered-one-of-many-ethics-questions-npr-must-an.

16. Ian Schwartz, "Seattle Mayor Durkan: CHAZ Has a 'Block Party Atmosphere,' Could Turn into 'Summer of Love,'" *Real Clear Politics,* June 12, 2020, www.realclearpolitics.com/video/2020/06/12/ seattle_mayor_durkan_chaz_has_a_block_party_atmosphere_could_turn_into_summer_of_ love.html. Also see "Blame Governor, Mayor for Violence in Portland," *Star Tribune,* September 4, 2020, www.startribune.com/blame-governor-mayor-for-violence-in-portland/572321732/.

17. "'We're Shutting You Down': Violent BLM Protesters Attack Stunned Diners and Smash Up a Restaurant in Rochester in Shocking Footage During Protest Over the Death of Daniel Prude," *Daily Mail UK,* September 7, 2020, www.dailymail.co.uk/news/article-8700321/Protesters-cause -diners-flee-panic-shut-restaurant-Rochester.html.

18. "Demonstrations Continue in LA in Response to the Death of George Floyd in Minnesota," *Los Angeles Times,* www.latimes.com/california/gallery/george-floyd-black-lives-matter-protesters -block-101-freeway.

19. Holly Matkin, "Motorist Left Unconscious in Street After Rioters Drag Him from Car and Beat Him," *Police Tribune*, August 9, 2020, https://policetribune.com/motorist-left-unconscious -in-street-after-rioters-drag-him-from-car-and-beat-him/.

20. Yaron Steinbuch, "Video Shows 'Antifa' Group Block Elderly Couple's Path, Yell 'Nazi Scum,'" *New York Post*, October 1, 2019, https://nypost.com/2019/10/01/video-shows-antifa-group-block -elderly-couples-path-yell-nazi-scum/.

21. Rzuelow, "Not a Single Negative Remark about Antifa from ANY Democrat," *C-Span*, August 4, 2020, www.c-span.org/video/?c4898088/user-clip-democrats-support-terrorist-antifa.

22. Steve Krakaue, "The Media Is Ignoring the Violence That's Tearing Our Cities Apart," *The Hill*, August 19, 2020, https://thehill.com/opinion/criminal-justice/512622-the-media-is-ignoring -the-violence-thats-tearing-our-cities-apart.

23. Mallory Simon, "Over 1,000 Health Professionals Sign a Letter Saying, Don't Shut Down Protests Using Coronavirus Concerns as an Excuse," *CNN*, June 5, 2020, www.cnn.com/2020/06/05/ health/health-care-open-letter-protests-coronavirus-trnd/index.html.

24. Bradley Cortright "Pelosi on Protesters Tearing Down Statues: 'People Will Do What They Do,'" *IJR*, July 9, 2020, https://ijr.org/pelosi-protesters-statues-people-will-do-what-they-do/.

25. "PragerU Takes Legal Action Against Google and YouTube for Discrimination," *PragerU*, www.prageru .com/press-release/prageru-takes-legal-action-against-google-and-youtube-for-discrimination/.

26. Jonathan Feldstein, "YouTube Flags CBN's Chris Mitchell's Prayer for Israel as 'Age Inappropriate," *CBN News*, November 3, 2020, www1.cbn.com/cbnnews/israel/2020/november/ youtube-flags-s-chris-mitchells-prayer-for-israel-as-age-inappropriate.

27. Michael W. Chapman, "How Social Media Giants Facebook, Twitter, YouTube Suppress Conservative Speech," *Yellow Hammer*, June 2017, https://yellowhammernews.com/ how-social-media-giants-facebook-twitter-youtube-suppress-conservative-speech/.

28. Ibid.

29. Ibid.

30. Ibid.

31. Edward Abbey, *Postcards from Ed: Dispatches and Salvos from an American Iconoclast* (Minneapolis, MN: Milkweed Editions, 2006).

32. "Videos of Pennsylvania Lawmaker Berating Pro-Life Demonstrators Spark Outrage."

33. Bill Maher commenting on Christianity and the Bible, www.goodreads.com/author/quotes/18481 .Bill_Maher.

34. Christian Today, "UK LGBT Activists Threaten to Burn Down Church, Attack Pastor Over Facebook Post," *Christian Post*, September 13, 2020, www.christianpost.com/news/uk-lgbt-activists -threaten-to-burn-church-violence-against-pastor-over-good-news-pride-canceled-post.html.

35. Warren Beatty and Trevor Griffiths, *Reds* (Paramount Pictures, 1981).

CHAPTER FOUR: YOU'VE BEEN STARRED

1. Christian Today, "UK LGBT Activists Threaten to Burn Down Church, Attack Pastor Over Facebook Post," *Christian Post*, September 13, 2020, www.christianpost.com/news/uk-lgbt-activists -threaten-to-burn-church-violence-against-pastor-over-good-news-pride-canceled-post.html.

2. Milton Kleg, "Anti-Semitism: Background to the Holocaust," www.socialstudies.org/sites/default/files/publications/se/5906/590605.html.

3. Corrie ten Boom with John and Elizabeth Sherrill, *The Hiding Place* (New York: Bantam Books, 1974).

4. "World Watch List," *Open Doors*, www.opendoorsusa.org/christian-persecution/world-watch-list/.

5. Kleg, "Anti-Semitism: Background to the Holocaust."

6. United States Holocaust Memorial Museum, "Antisemitic Legislation 1933–1939," *Holocaust Encyclopedia*, https://encyclopedia.ushmm.org/content/en/article/antisemitic-legislation-1933-1939.

7. Ibid.

8. Ibid.

9. Ibid.

10. Ibid.

11. Amy E. Swearer, "The ABA Is Against You and Other Things No One Tells Conservative or Christian Law Students," *Federalist Society*, February 14, 2018, https://fedsoc.org/commentary/fedsoc-blog/the-aba-is-against-you-and-other-things-no-one-tells-conservative-or-christian-law-students.

12. Albert E. Gunn and George O. Zenner, "Religious Discrimination in the Selection of Medical Students: A Case Study," *Linacre Quarterly*, vol. 63, no. 3, article 6, August 1996, https://epublications.marquette.edu/cgi/viewcontent.cgi?&article=2084&context=lnq. Also see: Matthew Clark, "Exposed: Christian Students Rejected, Failed, and Expelled for their Faith by State Colleges and Universities," *ACLJ*, https://aclj.org/religious-liberty/exposed-christian-students-rejected-failed-and-expelled-for-their-faith-by-state-colleges-and-universities.

13. Michael Foust, "Major LGBT Group Urges Biden to Strip Accreditation of Christian Schools, Colleges," *Christian Headlines,* November 19, 2020, www.christianheadlines.com/contributors/michael-foust/major-lgbt-group-urges-biden-to-strip-accreditation-of-christian-schools-colleges.html?utm_medium=fbpage&utm_source=Facebook&utm_campaign=cwupdate&fbclid=IwAR1RpgLihzcvaYMjuCCNHg0qbUIQOTwikdelo_0TeHk7TsTtbK7nFbtRmoE.

14. Eric Philips, "30-Year Military Chaplain Fired from Air Force—His Crime? Biblical Views on Sexual Morality," *CBN News*, November 30, 2020, www1.cbn.com/cbnnews/us/2020/november/30-year-military-chaplain-fired-from-air-force-ndash-his-crime-biblical-views-on-sexual-morality?fbclid=IwAR1s35PznkXzHUYnGe9GcCcTVbl_V5n-pvspH9wi2ZJy_08rILpWKBUVWuA.

15. Brandon Showalter, "Canadian City Calgary Bans 'Conversion Therapy,'" *Christian Post*, May 28, 2020, www.christianpost.com/news/canadian-city-calgary-bans-conversion-therapy.html.

16. Aila Slisco, "White Jesus Statues Should Be Torn Down, Activist Shaun King Says," *Newsweek,* June 22, 2020, www.newsweek.com/white-jesus-statues-should-torn-down-black-lives-matters-leader-says-1512674.

17. Valerie Richardson, "'No Place for God': Left-wing Protesters Turn Focus to Churches as Vandalism, Arson Escalate," *Washington Times*, July 15, 2020, www.washingtontimes.com/news/2020/jul/15/black-lives-matter-protesters-turn-rage-churches-r/. See also Michael Berry, "Antifa Rioters Target Catholic Church in Downtown Portland," Michael Berry blog, November 6, 2020, https://ktrh.iheart.com/featured/michael-berry/content/2020-11-06-antifa-rioters-target-catholic-church-in-downtown-portland/.

18. United States Holocaust Memorial Museum, "Book Burning," *Holocaust Encyclopedia*, https://encyclopedia.ushmm.org/content/en/article/book-burning.

19. See at https://twitter.com/LilaGraceRose/status/1125517225757007872?ref_src=twsrc%5Etfw%7Ctwcamp%5Etweetembed%7Ctwterm%5E1125749760575647744&ref_url=https%3A%2F%2Fwww.usatoday.com%2Fstory%2Fnews%2Fpolitics%2Fonpolitics%2F2019%2F05%2F07%2Fbrian-sims-pa-democratic-lawmaker-harasses-anti-abortion-activists%2F1127958001%2F.

20. Evan Sernoffsky, "Video Shows Man Kicking 85-year-old Antiabortion Demonstrator Outside Planned Parenthood in San Francisco," *San Francisco Chronicle*, March 27, 2019, www.sfchronicle.com/crime/article/Video-shows-man-kicking-85-year-old-antiabortion-13721975.php.

CHAPTER FIVE: WHY THE HOSTILITY?

1. Douglas O. Linder, "The Trial of Sir Thomas More: An Account," *UMKC School of Law*, https://famous-trials.com/thomasmore/986-home.

2. "World Watch List," Open Doors, www.opendoorsusa.org/christian-persecution/world-watch-list/.

3. Ibid.

4. Angelo Codevilla, "Revolution 2020," *American Mind*, September 23, 2020, https://americanmind.org/essays/revolution-2020/.

5. Edgar Allan Poe, "The Tell-Tale Heart," 1843, www.poemuseum.org/the-tell-tale-heart.

CHAPTER SIX: TEARS UNSHED

1. Lorraine Hansberry, *A Raisin in the Sun* (New York: Vintage Books, 1958).

2. Darcy Schild, "Stevie Nicks Says that if She Had Not Gotten an Abortion, She's 'Pretty Sure There Would Have Been No Fleetwood Mac,'" *Insider*, October 17, 2020, www.insider.com/stevie-nicks-abortion-fleetwood-mac-reproductive-rights-2020-10.

3. Keith L. Moore and T.V.N. Persaud, *The Developing Human: Clinically Oriented Embryology* (Philadelphia: W.B. Saunders Co., 1998), 77, 350 cited in Cathy Ruse and Rob Schwarzwalder, "The Best Pro-Life Arguments for Secular Audiences," Family Research Council, May 25, 2011, www.frc.org/brochure/the-best-pro-life-arguments-for-secular-audiences.

4. Ibid.

5. Emma Green, "Science Is Giving the Pro-Life Movement a Boost," *Atlantic*, January 18, 2018, www.theatlantic.com/politics/archive/2018/01/pro-life-pro-science/549308/.

6. Ibid.

7. Ibid.

8. Ibid.

9. "Feminist Foremothers," Feminists for Life of America, www.feministsforlife.org/herstory/.

10. "Legal Information Institute Supreme Court Resources: Roe v. Wade," *Oyez*, www.oyez.org/cases/1971/70-18.

11. Ibid.

12. Nicandro Iannacci, "Recalling the Supreme Court's Historic Statement on Contraception and Privacy," National Constitution Center, June 7, 2019, https://constitutioncenter.org/blog/contraception-marriage-and-the-right-to-privacy.

13. Ibid.

14. "Privacy," Legal Information Institute, www.law.cornell.edu/wex/privacy#:~:text=In%20Roe%2C%20the%20Supreme%20Court,state%20action%20.%20.%20.%20is%20broad.

15. Robert Marshall, "Reviving the Equal Rights Amendment to Keep Abortion Legal," *Charlotte Lozier Institute*, December 21, 2018, https://lozierinstitute.org/reviving-the-equal-rights-amendment-to-keep-abortion-legal/.

16. Ibid.

17. Sandra N. Bragg, "Abortions Performed to Preserve the Life or Health of the Mother," *OLR Research Report*, January 27, 2000, www.cga.ct.gov/2000/rpt/2000-R-0069.htm.

18. "Ethics Guide: Abortion in Self-Defence," *BBC*, 2014, www.bbc.co.uk/ethics/abortion/philosophical/selfdefence.shtml.

19. American Life League, "The Big Lie: Thousands of Illegal Abortion Deaths," *Eternal Word Television Network*, www.ewtn.com/catholicism/library/big-lie-thousand-of-illegal-abortion-deaths-9596.

20. Ibid.

21. Ibid.

22. Ibid.

23. Paul A. Specht, "Fact Check: 'Born Alive' Scenario Is Focus of NC Abortion Debate," *Raleigh News and Observer*, May 30, 2019, www.newsobserver.com/news/politics-government/article230992798.html.

24. Ibid.

25. Ibid.

26. Ibid.

27. "Women's Reasons for Having an Abortion," Guttmacher Institute Perspectives@50, 2020, www.guttmacher.org/perspectives50/womens-reasons-having-abortion#.

28. Maria Baer, "Abortion Regret Isn't a Myth, Despite New Study," *Christianity Today*, January 22, 2020, www.christianitytoday.com/news/2020/january/pro-life-abortion-regret-study-post-abortive-ministry.html.

29. "Voices of Women Who Mourn," *Feminists for Life of America*, www.feministsforlife.org/voices-of-women-who-mourn/.

30. Olivia Fleming, "'I Had an Abortion' T-Shirt Sparks Backlash at College, Students Wear 'I Haven't Killed a Baby' in Protest," *Daily Mail*, April 19, 2012, www.dailymail.co.uk/femail/article-2132138/I-abortion-T-shirts-spark-backlash-college-students-wear-I-havent-killed-baby-protest.html.

31. Corinne H. Rocca, Goleen Samari, Diana G. Foster, Heather Gould, Katrina Kimport, "Emotions and Decision Rightness Over Five Years Following an Abortion: An Examination of Decision Difficulty and Abortion Stigma," *Social Science and Medicine*, March 2020, www.sciencedirect.com/science/article/pii/S0277953619306999?via%3Dihub.

32. "Public Opinion on Abortion," Pew Research Center, August 29, 2019, www.pewforum.org/fact-sheet/public-opinion-on-abortion/.

33. "Abortion Trends by Gender," *Gallup*, https://news.gallup.com/poll/245618/abortion-trends-gender.aspx.

CHAPTER SEVEN: THE CROSS AND THE RAINBOW

1. *Obergefell et al. v. Hodges, Director, Ohio Department of Health, et al.*, Supreme Court of the United States, October Term, 2014, www.supremecourt.gov/opinions/14pdf/14-556_3204.pdf.

2. "California Assembly Passes Bill to Ban 'Conversion Therapy,'" *Equality California*, April 19, 2018, www.eqca.org/california-assembly-passes-bill-to-ban-conversion-therapy/.

3. Benjy Sarlin, "O'Rourke Says Churches Against Gay Marriage Should Lose Tax Benefits, Draws Backlash," *NBC News*, October 13, 2019, www.nbcnews.com/politics/2020-election/o-rourke-says-churches-against-gay-marriage-should-lose-tax-n1065186.

4. Jackson Elliott, "LGBT Group Urges Biden to Strip Accreditation of Christian Schools with Biblical Beliefs," *Christian Post*, November 20, 2020, www.christianpost.com/news/lgbt-group-urges-biden-to-force-christian-schools-to-capitulate.html.

5. "Assembly Concurrent Resolution No. 99," *California Legislative Information*, September 26, 2019, https://leginfo.legislature.ca.gov/faces/billTextClient.xhtml?bill_id=201920200ACR99.

6. "Americans' Moral Stance Towards Gay or Lesbian Relations in 2019," Statista Research Department, September 8, 2020, www.statista.com/statistics/225968/americans-moral-stance-towards-gay-or-lesbian-relations/.

7. "Just the Facts about Sexual Orientation and Youth," American Psychological Association, 2020, www.apa.org/pi/lgbt/resources/just-the-facts.

8. "Sexual Orientation and Homosexuality," American Psychological Association, 2008, www.apa.org/topics/lgbt/orientation.

9. Alia E. Dastagir, "'Born This Way'? It's Way More Complicated than That," *USA Today*, June 15, 2017, www.usatoday.com/story/news/2017/06/16/born-way-many-lgbt-community-its-way-more-complex/395035001/.

10. See Joe Dallas, *The Gay Gospel? How Pro-Gay Advocates Misread the Bible* (Eugene, OR: Harvest House Publishers, 2007).

11. "Max Lucado: The Beauty of Disagreeing Agreeably," Jen Hatmaker podcast, https://jenhatmaker.com/podcast/series-24/max-lucado-the-beauty-of-disagreeing-agreeably/.

12. Alisa Childers, "Max Lucado's Endorsement of Jen Hatmaker: What It Means and Why It Matters," January 13, 2020, www.alisachilders.com/blog/max-lucados-endorsement-of-jen-hatmaker-what-it-means-and-why-it-matters.

13. "Charles Spurgeon Quotes," *Brainy Quote*, www.brainyquote.com/authors/charles-spurgeon-quotes.

CHAPTER EIGHT: ETERNAL LIVES MATTER

1. "Racism," *Merriam-Webster* (Springfield, MA: Merriam-Webster, Inc., 2021), www.merriam-webster.com/dictionary/racism#note-1.

2. Ibid.

3. Ibid.

4. Lewis Carroll, *Through the Looking-Glass*, Bartleby, www.bartleby.com/73/2019.html.

5. Martin Luther King Jr., "I Have A Dream," American Rhetoric Top 100 Speeches, updated August 20, 2020, www.americanrhetoric.com/speeches/mlkihaveadream.htm.

6. "The Frankfurt School and Critical Theory," Marxist Internet Archives, www.marxists.org/subject/frankfurt-school/.

7. "Critical Theory: Social and Political Philosophy," *Encyclopedia Britannica*, 2020, www.britannica.com/topic/critical-theory.

8. Ibid.

9. Max Horkheimer, *Critical Theory* (New York: Seabury Press, 1972; reprinted New York: Continuum, 1982).

10. Chris Demaske, "Critical Race Theory," *First Amendment Encyclopedia*, 2009, www.mtsu.edu/first-amendment/article/1254/critical-race-theory.

11. Ibid.

12. "About Black Lives Matter," Black Lives Matter website, 2020, https://blacklivesmatter.com/about/.

13. Yaron Steinbuch, "Black Lives Matter Co-Founder Describes Herself as 'Trained Marxist,'" *New York Post*, June 25, 2020, https://nypost.com/2020/06/25/blm-co-founder-describes-herself-as-trained-marxist/.

14. "About Black Lives Matter," https://blacklivesmatter.com/about/.

15. "Black Lives Matter Co-Founders Patrisse Cullors, Alicia Garza, and Opal Tometi Named to TIME's Annual TIME100 List of the 100 Most Influential People in the World," Black Lives Matter website, September 23, 2020, https://blacklivesmatter.com/black-lives-matter-co-founders-patrisse-cullors-alicia-garza-and-opal-tometi-named-to-times-annual-time100-list-of-the-100-most-influential-people-in-the-world/.

16. Jason Rantz, "BLM's 'Mostly Peaceful' 93 Percent Study Sparks Renewed Propaganda," Opinion, *Newsweek*, September 8, 2020, www.newsweek.com/blms-mostly-peaceful-93-percent-study-sparks-renewed-propaganda-opinion-1529969.

17. Libby Emmons, "Exposed: BLM Quietly Scrubs Anti-American, Marxist Language from Its Website," Post Millennial.com, September 20, 2020, https://thepostmillennial.com/exposed-blm-quietly-scrubs-anti-american-marxist-language-from-its-website.

18. Demaske, "Critical Race Theory," *First Amendment Encyclopedia*.

19. "White Supremacy Groups in the United States," *The Counter Extremism Project*, https://www.counterextremism.com/content/us-white-supremacy-groups.

20. For example, see "UPS fires employee after being caught on camera in Milwaukee making racist remarks during delivery" *News 58*, January 6, 2021, https://www.cbs58.com/news/ups-fires-employee-after-being-caught-on-camera-in-milwaukee-making-racist-remarks-during-delivery See also Gage Goulding, "Lee County woman defends racist rant that was caught on camera," *NBC2 News*, January 26, 2021, https://nbc-2.com/news/2021/01/25/lee-county-woman-defends-racist-rant-that-was-caught-on-camera/.

21. For recent examples, see Janelle Griffith and Dennis Romero, "Cops fired over violent, racist talk about Black people: We are going to 'start slaughtering them,'" NBC News, June 25, 2020, https://www.nbcnews.com/news/us-news/cops-fired-over-violent-racist-talk-about-black -people-we-n1232072. See also "Cops' racist conversation caught on bodycam video," ABC News, January 30, 2021, https://abcnews.go.com/US/video/cops-racist-conversation-caught-bodycam -video-75584121.

CHAPTER NINE: MY BODY VS. MY SELF

1. Mark Mellman, "Mellman: Changing Views of Transgender Rights," *The Hill*, June 11, 2019, https://thehill.com/opinion/civil-rights/448047-mellman-changing-views-of-transgender-rights. In addition to an aggressively sympathetic entertainment and news media, the celebrity factor has also no doubt helped.

2. Rachel Savage, "Norway Outlaws Hate Speech Against Trans People," *Reuters*, November 25, 2020, www.reuters.com/article/norway-lgbt-lawmaking/norway-outlaws-hate-speech-against-trans -people-idUSKBN2852DL.

3. "How Many Adults Identify as Transgender in the United States?" UCLA School of Law Williams Institute, June 2016, https://williamsinstitute.law.ucla.edu/publications/trans-adults-united-states/.

4. Mere Abrams, "Is There a Difference Between Being Transgender and Transsexual?" *Healthline*, November 21, 2019, www.healthline.com/health/transgender/difference-between-transgender-and -transsexual#underlying-contention.

5. "DSM IV: Gender Identity Disorder," Gender Identity Disorder Today, *MH Today*, www.mental -health-today.com/gender/dsm.htm.

6. Alex Fradera, "Many Children and Teens with Gender Dysphoria Also Experience Mental Health Issues," *British Psychological Society*, January 17, 2018, https://digest.bps.org.uk/2018/01/17/ most-children-and-teens-with-gender-dysphoria-also-have-multiple-other-psychological-issues/.

7. Bioethics Observatory, "Causes of Transsexualism: Is There a Transsexuality Gene?" *Bioethics News Special Reports*, December 24, 2016, https://bioethicsobservatory.org/2016/12/is-there -transsexuality-gene/16389/.

8. Douglas Groothuis, "Gnosticism and the Gnostic Jesus," *Christian Research Journal*, April 21, 2009, www.equip.org/article/gnosticism-and-the-gnostic-jesus/.

9. "Voc #9 St. Augustine—Heresies," *Chegg Prep*, www.chegg.com/flashcards/voc-9-st-augustine -heresies-8a49d691-50db-4afe-bb6c-a3daede9b1d7/deck.

10. Stephen Hoeller, "The Gnostic World View: A Brief Summary of Gnosticism," *Gnostic Archive*, www.gnosis.org/gnintro.htm.

11. Katrina Rose, "The Transsexual and the Damage Done," file:///C:/Users/Renee/Downloads/2741 -Article%20Text-8975-1-10-20190718.pdf.

12. Colin Smothers, "Creation and Discrimination: Why the Male-Female Distinction Makes a Difference," CBMW.org, November 20, 2019, https://cbmw.org/2019/11/20/creation-and -discrimination-why-the-male-female-distinction-makes-a-difference/.

13. Paul McHugh, "Transgenderism: A Pathogenic Meme," *Public Discourse: A Journal of the Witherspoon Institute*, June 10, 2015, www.thepublicdiscourse.com/2015/06/15145/.

14. Ryan T. Anderson, PhD, "Sex Reassignment Doesn't Work. Here Is the Evidence," *Heritage Foundation*, March 9, 2018, www.heritage.org/gender/commentary/sex-reassignment-doesnt-work-here-the-evidence.

15. Ibid.

16. Ibid.

17. Ibid.

18. Ibid.

19. Ibid.

CHAPTER TEN: AN ORGY OF VIRTUE

1. "Woke," *Merriam-Webster Dictionary*, 2020, www.merriam-webster.com/dictionary/woke.

2. "Cancel culture," Dictionary.com, 2020, www.dictionary.com/e/pop-culture/cancel-culture/.

3. Rod Faulkner, "Newsflash: 'Social Justice Warrior' Is Not a Pejorative," *Noteworthy: The Journal Blog*, February 17, 2020, https://blog.usejournal.com/newsflash-social-justice-warrior-is-not-a-pejorative-8f2978d224e0.

4. "What Young Adults Say Is Missing," Barna Group, www.barna.com/research/missing-church/.

5. Hans Fiene, "Gay Marriage Isn't About Justice, It's About Selma Envy," *The Federalist*, March 31, 2015, https://thefederalist.com/2015/03/31/gay-marriage-isnt-about-justice-its-about-selma-envy/.

6. Andrew Sullivan, "America's New Religions," *New York*, December 7, 2018, https://nymag.com/intelligencer/2018/12/andrew-sullivan-americas-new-religions.html.

7. Jon Meacham, "Pastor Rob Bell: What if Hell Doesn't Exist?" *Time*, April 14, 2011, http://content.time.com/time/magazine/article/0,9171,2065289,00.html.

8. "The 8 Points of Progressive Christianity," Progressive Christianity.org, 2020, https://progressivechristianity.org/the-8-points/.

9. George Conger, "Presiding Bishop…'Jesus Is Not the Only Way to God,'" April 17, 2009, https://geoconger.wordpress.com/2009/04/17/presiding-bishop-jesus-is-not-the-only-way-to-god-cen-41709-p-7/.

10. Jonathan Merritt, "Oprah Finds Reasons to Believe," *Atlantic*, October 18, 2015, www.theatlantic.com/politics/archive/2015/10/oprah-finds-reasons-to-believe/411151/.

11. Neil Shenvi, "Social Justice, Critical Theory, and Christianity: Are They Compatible?" Lecture at Southeastern Baptist Theological Seminary, April 29, 2020, www.youtube.com/watch?v=E33aunwGQQ4.

12. Anna Skate, "The Trouble with Easter: How to (and not to) Talk to Kids About Easter," *Patheos: Unfundamentalist Parenting*, April 12, 2017, www.patheos.com/blogs/unfundamentalistparenting/2017/04/trouble-easter-not-talk-kids-easter/.

13. Ibid.

14. Natasha Crain, "Progressive Christianity Is as Much of a Threat to Your Kids' Faith as Atheism," *Natasha Crain*, June 1, 2017, https://natashacrain.com/progressive-christianity-is-as-much-of-a-threat-to-your-kids-faith-as-atheism/.

15. Alisa Childers, "5 Signs Your Church Might Be Heading Toward Progressive Christianity," *Alisa Childers*, May 8, 2017, www.alisachilders.com/blog/5-signs-your-church-might-be-heading -toward-progressive-christianity.

CHAPTER ELEVEN: ONE LAST STAND

1. "Elie Wiesel—Acceptance Speech," Nobel Prize, December 10, 1986, www.nobelprize.org/prizes/ peace/1986/wiesel/26054-elie-wiesel-acceptance-speech-1986/.

2. Albert Mohler, "The Scandal of Biblical Illiteracy: It's Our Problem," January 20, 2016, https:// albertmohler.com/2016/01/20/the-scandal-of-biblical-illiteracy-its-our-problem-4.

3. Alfred Adler, *Brainy Quote*, www.brainyquote.com/quotes/alfred_adler_106089.

4. David Nienhuis, "The Problem of Evangelical Biblical Illiteracy: A View from the Classroom," *Battle Cry*, July 24, 2013, https://thebattlecry49.com/2013/07/24/the-problem-of -evangelical-biblical-illiteracy-a-view-from-the-classroom-david-r-nienhuis/.

5. "Francis Schaeffer Quotes," *AZ Quotes*, www.azquotes.com/quote/718628.

6. Greg Bahnsen, quoted in *Penpoint Journal*, June 1991, 1.

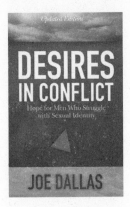

Desires in Conflict

This is the definitive "must-read" for those who wonder "Can a homosexual change?" This new edition with updated information offers more compelling reasons why the answer is yes. A thoroughly biblical and compassionate resource.

When Homosexuality Hits Home

No matter the relationship—the admission from a family member who says, "I'm gay" will likely mark a change in the way you and your loved one understand each other. These can be difficult waters to navigate, but Joe knows the rough waters firsthand and offers answers to the questions you need answered.

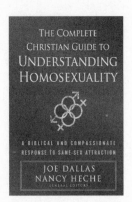

The Complete Christian Guide to Understanding Homosexuality

This well-researched and highly readable guide is the perfect go-to manual for families, church workers, counselors, pastors, civic leaders, schools, and those who themselves struggle with same-sex attraction.

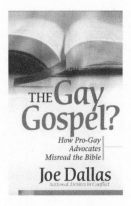

The Gay Gospel?

Helps readers to understand what pro-gay theology is and how to respond to it in a biblical manner.

We Will Not Be Silenced
Erwin W. Lutzer

Each day, you watch America turn further from Christian values and the core principles of liberty. It's frustrating to feel you can't assert biblical truth without facing condemnation, and frightening to witness outrage and victimhood replace respect and reason. Amidst this dissent, how can you not only stay rooted in your faith but continue to publicly testify for Jesus?

We Will Not Be Silenced will help prepare you to live out your convictions against a growing tide of hostility. Gain a better understanding of nonbelievers' legitimate hurts and concerns regarding issues like racism, sexism, and poverty—and identify the toxic responses secular culture disguises as solutions. In the process, you'll see how you can show compassion and gentleness to those outside of the faith without affirming their beliefs.

We Will Not Be Silenced will ready you to move beyond fear and boldly accept the challenge of representing Christ to a watching world that needs Him now more than ever before.

To learn more about Harvest House books and
to read sample chapters, visit our website:

www.harvesthousepublishers.com

HARVEST HOUSE PUBLISHERS
EUGENE, OREGON